JavaScript for

Sound Artists

Learn to Code with the Web Audio API

JavaScript for

Sound Artists

Learn to Code with the Web Audio API

Authored by: **William Turner**

Edited by: **Steve Leonard**

CRC Press
Taylor & Francis Group
Boca Raton London New York

CRC Press is an imprint of the
Taylor & Francis Group, an **informa** business

CRC Press
Taylor & Francis Group
6000 Broken Sound Parkway NW, Suite 300
Boca Raton, FL 33487-2742

© 2017 by Taylor & Francis Group, LLC
CRC Press is an imprint of Taylor & Francis Group, an Informa business

No claim to original U.S. Government works

Printed on acid-free paper
Version Date: 20161208

International Standard Book Number-13: 978-1-138-96153-1 (Paperback)

Library of Congress Cataloging-in-Publication Data

Names: Turner, William (Web site developer), author. | Leonard, Steve
(Web site developer), author.
Title: JavaScript for sound artists : learn to code with the Web Audio API /
William Turner, Steve Leonard.
Description: Boca Raton : Taylor & Francis, CRC Press, 2017.
Identifiers: LCCN 2016032832| ISBN 9781138961531 (pbk. : alk. paper) |
ISBN 9781138731134 (hardback : alk. paper)
Subjects: LCSH: Computer sound processing. | JavaScript (Computer program
language) | Webcasting.
Classification: LCC TK7881.4 .T87 2017 | DDC 006.5--dc23
LC record available at https://lccn.loc.gov/2016032832

Visit the Taylor & Francis Web site at
http://www.taylorandfrancis.com

and the CRC Press Web site at
http://www.crcpress.com

Printed in Canada.

Contents

Preface   xv

Acknowledgment   xix

I. Overview and Setup   I

What Is a Program?...1
What Is JavaScript? 1
HTML, CSS, and JavaScript...2
What Is a Web Application?..3
What Is the Web Audio API?..3
Setting Up Your Work Environment 4
    Setup View in Browser for Windows.....................................6
    Setup View in Browser for Mac 6
How to Create Code Snippets 6
Accessing the Chrome Developer Tools...7
Troubleshooting Problems and Getting Help 8

2. Getting Started with JavaScript and the Web Audio API   9

Hello Sound Program 9
Variables 10
null 12
Documenting Your Code with Comments 12
Exploring Variables with an Oscillator 12
console.log() 13
String 14
    Built-In String Methods. 15
        toUpperCase() 15
        toLowerCase() 15
        charAt() 15
        replace() 16
        slice() 16
The length Property. 17
Numbers 17
    How to Determine the Data Type of a Variable. 17
    Examples of Arithmetic Operators 18
    Examples of Precedence. 18
    Math.min() and Math.max(). 19
    Math.ceil() and Math.floor() 19
    Math.random(). 19
    Math.abs(). 20
Number-to-String Conversion. 20
Arrays. 20
    push(). 21
    pop() 21
    shift() 22
    unshift(). 22
    concat() 22
Summary. 22

3. Operators   23

What Are Operators?. 23
    Assignment Operators. 24
        Assignment. 24
        Addition Assignment 24
        Subtraction Assignment. 25
        Multiplication Assignment 25
        Division Assignment. 25
        Modulo Assignment 25
    The Boolean Data Type 25
    Comparison Operators 26
        Equality Operator 26

Strict Equality Operator...27
Greater Than and Less Than Operators........................27
Greater Than or Equal to Operator...........................27
Less Than or Equal to Operator 28
Not Equal to Operator 28
Strict Not Equal to Operator 28
Logical Operators 28
The Logical AND Operator 29
The Logical OR Operator 29
The NOT Operator 29
Summary..30

4. Conditional Statements and Loops   31

Conditional Statements..................................31
The if Statement 32
The switch Statement 33
Ternary Operator 34
Loops 35
for Loops 35
Using for Loops with Arrays......................36
while Loops..37
When to Use for Loops and When to Use while Loops 38
Summary..38

5. Functions   39

Functions—A Simple Example 39
Parts of a Function 40
Function Expressions................................41
Abstracting Oscillator Playback......................41
A Working Effects Box Example 42
The Arguments Object...............................43
Function Scope...44
Why You Should Always Declare Your Variables with var............46
Variable Hoisting 46
How Hoisting Affects Functions 47
Anonymous Functions 48
Closures...49
What Is a Closure? 49
Callback Functions 52
Working with JavaScript's Built-In Callback Functions..............53
filter()...53
map() 53
Recursion..54
Summary..55

6. Objects   57

JavaScript Data Types 57
Looping through Objects 59
When to Use Objects Rather Than Arrays 60
How to Check If an Object Has Access to a
Particular Property or Method 60
Cloning Objects 60
Prototypal Inheritance 61
The "this" Keyword 61
The bind Function 62
Summary 64

7. Node Graphs and Oscillators   65

The AudioContext() Method 65
Node Graphs 66
Oscillators 66
The stop Method 67
The onended Property 67
How to Stop Oscillators and Restart Them 67
The type Property 68
The frequency Property 69
The detune Property 69
Summary 69

8. Using HTML and CSS to Build User Interfaces   71

What Is a User Interface? 71
    HTML 71
Explanation of the HTML Template 72
Understanding HTML Elements 73
Form and Input Elements 76
    CSS 77
Comments 79
Element Selectors 79
Grouping Selectors 80
Descendent Selectors 80
Child Selectors 80
class and id 81
Modifying the App Interface 81
Margin, Border, and Padding 84
Removing List Element Bullet Points 86
Font Size, Style (Type), and Color 86
Centering Block-Level Elements 87
Summary 89

9. DOM Programming with JavaScript   91

How Does JavaScript Communicate with the DOM? 91
  HTML. 91
  JavaScript 92
Building the Application. 93
How to Trigger an Oscillator by Clicking a Button 93
Toggling the *Start/Stop* Text. 94
Programming the Frequency Slider 96
Changing the Frequency in Real Time. 97
Changing Waveform Types 99
Completed Code with Waveform Selection. 100
Giving an Outline to the Selected Waveform Type 101
Summary. 102

10. Simplifying DOM Programming with JQuery   103

What Is JQuery?. 103
JQuery Setup 103
Referencing JQuery Directly 104
Using JQuery from a CDN 104
How to Use JQuery 105
Selecting HTML Elements 105
Storing DOM Selectors as Variables. 105
Using Methods. 106
  HTML. 106
  JQuery/JavaScript to Change a Single Property. 106
  JQuery/JavaScript to Change Multiple Properties. 107
Method Chaining. 107
  HTML. 107
  CSS 107
  JQuery/JavaScript 107
  HTML. 108
  JQuery/JavaScript 108
The this Keyword 108
  HTML. 108
  JQuery/JavaScript 108
Refactoring the Oscillator Player to Use JQuery. 108
  Without JQuery. 109
  With JQuery. 109
Setting Up the Event Listener for the User-Selected List Element 110
  Event Listener without JQuery 110
  Event Listener with JQuery. 111
Modifying the Code in setInterval 111
  setInterval Method without JQuery. 111
  setInterval Method with JQuery. 112

onOff Method without JQuery...................................112
$onOff Selector with JQuery 112
Summary...113

11. Loading and Playing Audio Files   115

Prerequisites 115
The Two Steps to Loading an Audio File 116
The XMLHttpRequest Object 117
    get Requests...117
A Word on Audio File Type Compatibility 118
Synchronous *versus* Asynchronous Code Execution.................118
Processing the Audio Buffer with the Node Graph 120
Summary...120

12. Factories and Constructors   121

JavaScript and the Concept of *Class* 121
What Are Classes?..122
The Factory Pattern..122
Dynamic Object Extension.....................................123
Private Data...124
Getters and Setters...124
Constructors and the new Keyword.............................125
Adding Methods to Constructors...............................126
The Prototype Object and the Prototype Property.................126
Why Do Constructors Exist If You Can Do the Same
Thing with Factories? 128
Summary...128

13. Abstracting the File Loader   129

Thinking about Code Abstraction 129
Creating the Abstraction 130
Walking through the Code.....................................132
Summary...135

14. The Node Graph and Working with Effects   137

How to *Think About* the Node Graph...........................137
Gain Nodes 138
The Placement of Nodes Is Up to You..........................139
What Effects Are Available?....................................139
How to Determine the Nodes You Need to
Create the Effect You Want....................................140

A Real-World Example 141
Some Effects Require Development Work 141
Summary 142

15. The Biquad Filter Node   143

Using the Biquad Filter Node 143
Filter Types 144
Creating an Equalizer 146
Graphic EQ 146
Parametric EQ 148
Summary 149

16. The Convolver Node   151

Convolution Reverb 151
Where to Get Pre-Recorded Impulse Response Files 152
Using Impulse Response Files 152
  HTML 153
  JavaScript 153
Controlling the Amount of Reverberation 154
Summary 155

17. Stereo Panning, Channel Splitting, and Merging   157

The Stereo Panner Node 157
The Channel Splitter 158
The Channel Merger 159
Merging All Channels of a Multichannel File into
a Single Mono Channel 159
Using the Merger and Splitter Nodes Together 160
Summary 160

18. The Delay Node   161

The Delay Node 161
Creating Echo Effects 162
Creating Slap Back Effects 162
Creating a Ping-Pong Delay 163
Summary 164

19. Dynamic Range Compression   165

The Dynamics Compressor Node 165
Summary 167

20. Time   169

The Timing Clock 169
The `start` Method...170
Looping Sounds 170
Update Your Audio Loader Library 171
Changing Audio Parameters over Time...............................171
The Audio Parameter Methods 172
    The `setValueAtTime` Method................................172
    The `exponentialRampToValueAtTime` Method 172
    The `linearRampToValueAtTime` Method 173
    The `setTargetAtTime()` Method 173
    The `setValueCurveAtTime()` Method 173
Summary...174

21. Creating Audio Visualizations   175

A Brief Word on Fourier Analysis..................................175
A Brief Explanation of Binary-Coded Decimal Numbers...............176
The Spectrum Analyzer 176
    JavaScript/JQuery 176
    HTML...177
    CSS 178
Walking through the Code..179
Storing the Frequency Data in an Array 180
How to *Think About* the `frequencyData` Array 181
    Building the Display Interface 181
Connecting the Analyzer to the DOM................................182
Summary...183

22. Adding Flexibility to the Audio Loader Abstraction   185

The Updated Interface...185
Modifying the Library...186
Modifying `audioBatchLoader`......................................188
An Explanation of the Previous Code Edit 188
Summary...189

23. Building a Step Sequencer   191

The Problem 191
Can I Use `setInterval` or `setTimeout`?..........................192
The Solution 193
How It Works 193
Changing Tempo 195
Building the Sequencer 196

Playing Back Sounds in Sequence 197
Creating the User Interface Grid. 202
   HTML. 202
   CSS 203
Adding Interactivity to the Grid Elements 205
Summary. 206

24. AJAX and JSON 207

AJAX 207
JSON. 208
Making an AJAX Call to the iTunes Search API 208
How the Code Works 209
   HTML. 210
   JavaScript 210
Creating Your Own Web API to Reference Synthesizer Patch Data 210
The Data Structure. 213
   HTML. 213
   CSS 214
How the Code Works 216
Building on the API. 217
   data.js. 217
   module.js 218
Extend the JSON Object 219
Summary. 220

25. The Future of JavaScript and the Web Audio API 221

The Web Audio API 1.0. 221
   3D Spacial Positioning. 221
Raw Modification of Audio Buffer Data. 222
Suggestions for Continued Learning 222
   JavaScript 6 222
   node.js. 223
   The Web MIDI API. 223
   Open Sound Control 223
Summary. 223
Further Reading. 223
Book Website 223

Index 225

Preface

Learning to program can be daunting, and we want to be the first to congratulate you for taking on the challenge! Second, we want to thank you for choosing this book.

▐▌ Who Is This Book For?

This book is for anyone who is involved in the world of creative audio and wants to learn to program using the JavaScript language. There are many programming books directed toward artists to help them build websites, mobile applications, games, and other things, but next to none is directed exclusively toward the sound arts community. This book is designed to fill this role and to teach the fundamentals of web-based software development, and specifically, the basics of the JavaScript programming language to *sound artists*.

▐▌ What This Book Is *Not*

This book is not an audio technology reference. It does not take the time to explain the fundamentals of audio theory or sound engineering in depth. Words and phrases like *dynamic range compression*, *convolution reverb*, and *sample rate* are thrown around like candy with only a cursory explanation (if they are explained at all). We assume that you are either familiar with many of these core audio concepts or know enough to find the answers on your own. If you need an accommodating audio technology reference, we suggest David Miles Huber's excellent book *Modern Recording Techniques*, Taylor & Francis.

This book is also not directed toward experienced programmers who are simply interested in JavaScript or the Web Audio API. If this describes you, then you may find *some* value here, but you are not the intended audience.

How to Learn to Program

The following are a few tips to help you get the most from this book.

Make Connections

Generally, it is easier to learn new things by making associations and connections to areas that you are already familiar with. If you have ever programmed a synth or a MIDI sequencer, then you have already done a *form* of programming. The contents of this book are designed to be a bridge that connects a world you are (presumably) familiar with (sound and audio technology) to a topic you are less familiar with—JavaScript and programming. We suggest that you tap into whatever has drawn you to sound art while learning the material in this book.

Flow and Frustration Are *Not* Opposites

It's very important to embrace a sense of flow when learning to program. It is also important to embrace frustration *as part of the flow state* and not as the antithesis of it. When you learn something new, the neurons in your brain are making connections; this may physically feel like frustration, but it just means your brain is rewiring—literally. Embrace this.

Make It Habitual

Programming is all about learning a bunch of little things that combine to make big things. The best way to learn a lot of little things is through repetition and habit. One way to do this is to simply accept programming as a new part of your lifestyle and do a little bit (or a lot) every day.

Be Creative and Have Personal Projects

It is a good idea to have your own personal programming projects. The more you are personally invested in a project, the more you will learn.

Talk and Teach

One of the best ways to validate your own learning is to teach someone else. If you don't have anyone to teach, then you can substitute this by writing tutorials. This will force you to collect your thoughts and express them clearly.

Keep Going

Our final piece of advice is to simply *stick with it*.
Best of luck!
If you have any questions or comments, you can find us at:
http://www.javascriptforsoundartists.com

William Turner
Steve Leonard

Acknowledgment

Thanks to technical assistant Keith Oppel.

1 Overview and Setup

▎▌ What Is a Program?

A program is any set of instructions that is created or followed. In this book, we focus on writing computer programs, which are lists of instructions that a computer carries out. These instructions can be written and stored in various forms. Some of the first modern computers used punched cards, switches, and cables. Early analog music synthesizers were a type of computer that used a patchbay style interface to manually allow a programmer to create specific sounds.

▎▌ What Is JavaScript?

JavaScript is a multipurpose programming language initially created to aid developers in adding dynamic features to websites. The language was initially created in 11 days and released in 1995 by a company called Netscape. Developed by Brendan Eich, its original release name was LiveScript. When Netscape introduced support for the language in its browser, LiveScript was renamed JavaScript. Although JavaScript is similar in name to the Java programming language, they are completely unrelated. Today, JavaScript is used in everything from robotics to home automation systems.

▌ HTML, CSS, and JavaScript

The three main technologies used to build websites and web applications are HTML, CSS, and JavaScript.

HTML stands for *hypertext markup language* and is the standard by which we create documents for the World Wide Web. You program HTML by writing elements (sometimes referred to as tags for brevity). These elements contain text and other nested elements, which make up the document's content.

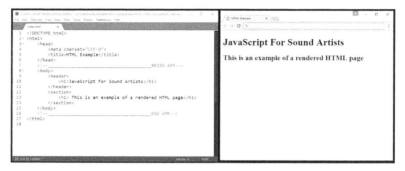

CSS stands for *cascading style sheets* and is a tool used to modify how HTML elements and text are presented. CSS is primarily a visual design tool. For example, with CSS you could modify an HTML element and give it an orange background, change its font size, place it vertically or horizontally, or perform any number of creative visual changes.

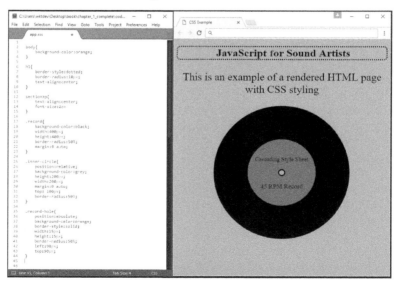

JavaScript is used to add interactive responses to user input. Every time a user clicks, scrolls, taps, moves the mouse cursor, types, or performs an interactive event, JavaScript code can be triggered to change the page in some manner.

The JavaScript language was initially designed to perform these functions within the context of designing websites and applications.

What Is a Web Application?

A web application is any website that contains more than static, non-interactive pages. This means that, in a web application, the pages have some interactive components in addition to the static text and images displayed. In the early days of the World Wide Web, websites were composed mostly of collections of static documents connected through highlighted text called hyperlinks. These static pages had no interaction with databases. In the early 1990s, this began to change, and web developers began creating websites that had features similar to desktop applications that allowed users to interact with the page via form fields, buttons, and other interactive means to send data over a web server to and from a database.

Early web applications were slow and limited by the technology of the time. In the early 2000s, a culmination of technical shifts that included client-side- rather than server-side-focused web applications helped make web applications more responsive. Part of this shift is attributable to a technology called AJAX (asynchronous JavaScript and XML). This technology pushed dynamic web application development forward by allowing the browser to retrieve and send data to a web server without having to automatically refresh the page in the process. As the J in AJAX indicates, JavaScript is central to this technology, and web applications began to approach the interactive speed of their desktop counterparts.

As you might expect, within the audio world there were attempts to leverage this new technology, which resulted in browser-based audio players, editors, and musical instruments. Many of these applications were initially written using a technology called Flash. This is a proprietary technology that required the user to download and install an additional plug-in to run all programs written in it.

In 2008, a newer version of the HTML standard was written, called HTML-5. This version included an audio player that could directly stream sound files off a web server using a single line of HTML code. The player also included built-in, user-facing controls for play, fast-forward, rewind, pause, stop, loop, and other actions. However, for serious audio development, this was inadequate. Web application developers and audio aficionados wanted something more fully featured.

What Is the Web Audio API?

The Web Audio API is a series of exposed code pieces that you can use to accomplish musical and audio tasks in a web browser with less effort than if you were to create them all from scratch. The unexposed portion of the Web Audio API lies in the web browser's source code and is written in whatever language the web browser itself is written in. The technical core of web browsers is usually written in multiple lower-level languages, which can include (but are not limited to) C++, Java, and machine language.

To understand the Web Audio API, you must first understand what an API is. API stands for *application programming interface*. An API is a portion of code that a programmer is given access to, which controls a larger unseen body of code within certain constraints. Imagine if, in order to learn how to play your favorite musical instrument, you had to literally build it from scratch. As you can imagine, this would get very tedious—especially if the instrument were to break. Thus, it's much more convenient to learn to play a premade musical instrument. The convenience here is that the construction process is removed and your only concern is what is important to you, which is the controls needed to use the instrument. In a similar manner, programmers write APIs that expose only small pieces of code for developers to use, and these small pieces of code allow you to do a lot of work with minimal effort.

In addition to being able to load and play back sound files, the Web Audio API also allows you to generate sound from scratch in the form of oscillators. You can then manipulate any sound playback or generation using filters, reverb effects, dynamic compressors, delay effects, and a host of other options.

Setting Up Your Work Environment

To begin working, you must first determine what browser you are going to troubleshoot with. In real-world environments, you would use a test suite to troubleshoot among different browsers and platforms. In this book, we are going to keep things simple and only use Google Chrome. The next thing you need is a code editor. For the exercises, we assume you will be using the Sublime Text editor. Technically, you can use any code editor you want, but Sublime Text is offered as a free trial download and is extremely powerful and widely used. We think it's worth your investment of time to learn it.

The next thing you need to do is create a folder with a basic work template.

1. If you are not already using it, go to this URL to download and install Google Chrome: https://www.google.com/chrome/browser/desktop/.

2. Go to http://www.sublimetext.com/ and download and install Sublime Text.

3. Create a folder on your desktop or in a directory and call it *web audio template*.

4. Open Sublime Text, and in the window that appears, type the following code into it. Then save the file (go to the File menu in Sublime Text and click *Save As*) as *index.html* and choose your *web audio template* folder as the directory to save it in.

```
<!DOCTYPE html>
<html>
  <head>
    <meta charset="UTF-8">
    <title>app</title>
    <script src="js/app.js"></script>
    <link rel="stylesheet" href="css/app.css">
  </head>
  <!--_____BEGIN APP-->
  <body>

  </body>
  <!--_____END APP-->
</html>
```

5. Inside the web audio template folder, create another folder called css.

6. In Sublime Text, create a new file by going to the File menu and click *New*. Save this file in your css folder as app.css. Leave the contents of this file empty.

7. In the web audio template folder, create another folder called js.

8. Create a new empty document in Sublime Text, then type "use strict"; (including quotations and semicolon) at the top of it and save it as app. js in the js folder you just created. This places your JavaScript in strict mode. Strict mode is a restrictive form of JavaScript that enforces better programming practices. All JavaScript code examples in this book will assume you have strict mode enabled.

You are now going to add a few extensions to Sublime Text that will make working with the editor easier in the long term. To do this, you must first download and install the package manager plug-in. Go to the following link and follow the directions on the left side of the window: https://packagecontrol.io/installation. When done, close the console by entering the keys: Ctrl + ` (apostrophe, on the key with the ~).

1. In the Sublime Text menu, go to *Tools > Command Palette*, and in the form field that appears, type install. You should see an option menu appear that says *Package control: Install package*. Click this menu option.

2. Another form field with a series of options appears. This form field allows you to search and explore various plug-ins for Sublime Text. You are now going to install a plug-in that allows you to create a local web server that will be necessary when working with audio files. In the form field, type Sublime server. A list of search results should appear. Click the first one. Look at the bottom of the Sublime Text window, and you

should see "installing" in small text. When this process is done, quit and restart Sublime Text. We will cover the specifics of the web server in a later chapter. But rest assured that this setup will be time well spent. To verify that the plug-in is installed, go to *Tools > SublimeServer > Start SublimeServer*. Open your web browser to http://localhost:8080/, and it should display *SublimeServer* at the top of the page.

3. This last plug-in you are going to install lets you open HTML files in Chrome from *within* Sublime Text. To install the View in Browser plug-in, go to *Tools > Command Palette* and in the form field that appears, type `install`. Click *Package control: Install package*. Then do a search for *View in Browser*, and select the first option that appears. Once the installation is done, you will need to go to the following menu to set up the plug-in to work with Chrome.

Setup View in Browser for Windows

In Sublime Text, go to the *Preferences* menu and click *Package Settings*. Look for the *View in Browser* menu item, hover over it, and select *Settings – Default*. Select all the code you see and copy it. You are now going to paste it into the *Settings – User* page of the same plug-in. So go back to the *Preferences* menu and select *Package Settings > View in Browser > Settings – User*. Paste all the code you just copied into this window. At the very bottom, you should see a line of code that says *"browser": "firefox"*. Change the word *firefox* to either *chrome*, or *chrome64* if you have a 64-bit operating system. It should look like this: *"browser": "chrome"* or *"browser": "chrome64"*. If you open an empty document in Sublime Text and use the key command Ctrl + Alt + V, Chrome should launch and open that page.

Setup View in Browser for Mac

As soon as the plug-in is downloaded, you should be able to open an empty Sublime Text document in Chrome using the key command Control + Option + C.

I▌ How to Create Code Snippets

It can be helpful to know how to create code snippets that you can access without writing them out character-by-character every time. Thankfully, Sublime Text has a feature that allows you to do this with snippets. To create a snippet, do the following steps:

1. In Sublime Text menu, go to *Tools > New Snippet*.

2. In the window that appears, delete everything on line 3 and paste the following text: `This is a test snippet`.

```
untitled • (html_css_example, hello sound) - Sublime Text                    —    □    ×
File  Edit  Selection  Find  View  Goto  Tools  Project  Preferences  Help
    untitled          ●
 1  <snippet>
 2      <content><![CDATA[
 3  Hello, ${1:this} is a ${2:snippet}.
 4  ]]></content>
 5      <!-- Optional: Set a tabTrigger to define how to trigger the snippet -->
 6      <!-- <tabTrigger>hello</tabTrigger> -->
 7      <!-- Optional: Set a scope to limit where the snippet will trigger -->
 8      <!-- <scope>source.python</scope> -->
 9  </snippet>
10
Line 7, Column 46                                          Tab Size: 4       XML
```

3. On line 6, remove the <!-- and --> characters and type the word test in between the two elements. The result should look like this: *<tabTrigger>test</tabTrigger>*.

```
untitled • (html_css_example, hello sound) - Sublime Text                    —    □    ×
File  Edit  Selection  Find  View  Goto  Tools  Project  Preferences  Help
    untitled          ●
 1  <snippet>
 2      <content><![CDATA[
 3  This is a test snippet
 4  ]]></content>
 5      <!-- Optional: Set a tabTrigger to define how to trigger the snippet -->
 6      <tabTrigger>test</tabTrigger>
 7      <!-- Optional: Set a scope to limit where the snippet will trigger -->
 8      <!-- <scope>source.python</scope> -->
 9  </snippet>
10
Line 10, Column 1                                          Tab Size: 4       XML
```

4. Save the file in the default directory that appears and call it *test. sublime-snippet*.

5. Open your *index.html* file in Sublime Text, type the word test, then tap the TAB button on your keyboard. The phrase "this is a test snippet" should appear in the editor.

▮▮ Accessing the Chrome Developer Tools

Google Chrome has a built-in suite of troubleshooting tools called the Chrome Developer Tools. You can access these tools by opening the browser and using the key commands:

Windows OS or Linux: Ctrl + Shift + J

Mac: Command + Option + J

We are not going to go over the utility of the developer tools just yet, but they will be highlighted throughout the book.

Troubleshooting Problems and Getting Help

If you have any trouble, try using search engines to research solutions. One very good resource is http://stackoverflow.com, which is a community of programmers who ask and answer questions. They have a nice section on JavaScript as well as a lively Web Audio API community that you can find at: http://stackoverflow.com/questions/tagged/web-audio.

2 Getting Started with JavaScript and the Web Audio API

▌ Hello Sound Program

In an introduction to a programming language, the first program you write is often called "Hello World," which prints the words "Hello World" on the screen. Because we are using the Web Audio API to create sounds, this section explains how to create a "Hello Sound" application that immediately plays a sound when you run it.

Copy the folder *web audio template* from the last chapter to a new directory, and rename the copy to *hello_sound*.

Type the code below into the *app.js* file that is present within the *hello_sound* folder. Save it and then launch the *index.html* file from your web browser. You should hear a basic sine wave oscillator playing.

```
var audioContext = new AudioContext();
var osc = audioContext.createOscillator();
osc.type = "sine";
osc.connect(audioContext.destination);
osc.start(audioContext.currentTime);
```

After you verify that the Hello Sound program works, close the browser. You just wrote your first Web Audio API program!

The code you just ran is a basic oscillator generation and playback script. The first line in the script is called the "Audio Context" and this tells the browser that you are using the Web Audio API. The next line of code creates an oscillator. The third line of code assigns a waveform type to the oscillator, whereas line four connects the oscillator to a virtual audio output called the *destination*, which is analogous to the speakers of your computer. The last line starts the oscillator playing. We will cover detailed operation of the Web Audio API in future chapters. First, though, we need to cover the basics of the JavaScript language.

▌ Variables

One of the first steps in writing a program is understanding variables and variable assignment. Variables are word forms that are used to store data. For example:

```
var waveformType = "sawtooth";
```

The variable here is named `waveformType`. This is preceded by the `var` keyword. You always specify the `var` keyword prior to declaring the variable. *Declaring* a variable means you are *creating a new variable*. After the `var` keyword, you type a space and give a name to your variable. Variable names are typically a reflection of something they represent. In this case, the variable is being used to describe a type of oscillator waveform and so is named `waveformType`. You probably noticed the odd capitalization of the word "type" in `waveformType`. The convention of capitalizing words to distinguish them within variable names is called *camel case*. This convention is used because variable names cannot contain white space to separate them. If you rewrote the variable in the following manner, you get an error:

```
var waveform type = "sawtooth"; //____returns an error
```

Type the above code into the *app.js* file of your *hello_sound* template. Launch Chrome and open the developer tools (Windows: Ctrl + Shift + J or Mac: Command + Option + J). Inside the console tab, you should see an error similar to the one in the following image.

The text in gray is the actual error and is identified as a syntax error. To the right of the error, you can see the file and the line number where the error occurred. This number corresponds to the line number in your file, which might differ from the one in the image. After you see the error, remove the line you added that is causing the error in *app.js* and save the file.

After you declare and name a variable, you can assign some data to it. You use the assignment operator "=" to do this.

It is important to understand that in JavaScript the "=" symbol is not called the *equal sign* and its functionality *does not* mean *equal to*. The "=" symbol indicates assignment, so it is called the *assignment operator*. The value on the right side of the assignment operator contains the data you want to assign to the variable name on the left side. In the following example, the string `"sawtooth"` is assigned to the variable `waveformType`.

```
var waveformType = "sawtooth";
```

When you assign a string of words to a variable, you must place them between quotation marks. The resulting data type is called a `string`. Data types represent the types of data that you can use in your program. Different programming languages have different data types. JavaScript has six data types, and one of these is the *string* data type (see Chapter 6 for a list of JavaScript data types).

After you assign data to your variable, you must end the variable declaration with a semicolon.

In summary, there are five parts to a variable declaration:

- The `var` keyword

- The variable name

- The assignment operator

- The data you wish to assign to the variable

- The closing semicolon

You can assign multiple variables at once using the following syntax:

```
var osc1 = 1200,
    osc2 = 1300,
    osc3 = 100;
```

In some cases, you might want to declare a variable and not assign data to it, as in the following example:

```
var waveformType;
```

If you do this, JavaScript automatically assigns `undefined` to it. You can also assign `undefined` explicitly like this:

```
var waveformType = undefined;
```

The keyword `undefined` is another JavaScript data type. Notice that `undefined` is not enclosed in quotation marks because it is not a string but represents a data type.

null

The primitive value `null` is similar to the primitive value `undefined`. Both can act as a placeholder for empty variables. When the `typeof` operator (discussed later in this chapter) is used to determine the type of `null`, the result is `object`. This is not what you might expect and is a flaw in the language. The correct returned value should be `null`. Because of this, we suggest that you never use `null` and always use `undefined`.

Documenting Your Code with Comments

When you are programming, it is a good habit to type messages into your code that are intended to be read by human beings (yourself or others) and not be interpreted by the computer. These messages are called *comments*. You can write either single-line or multiline comments in your program, and they look like this:

```
//This is a single line comment.
//It begins with two forward slash characters
//These end at the end of the line
/* This is a multi-line comment and begins with a forward slash
  and asterisk. It ends with an asterisk and a forward slash */
```

In a real-world scenario, we might comment our code like this:

```
var waveformType = "sawtooth"; // oscillator variable
```

All the characters from the `//` to the end of the line are ignored by the computer.

Exploring Variables with an Oscillator

Now that you understand what variables are, the following example shows how you use them.

Open up the code you wrote at the beginning of this chapter, and add the variable `waveformType` to it, as in the following code:

```
var audioContext = new AudioContext();
var waveformType = "sawtooth"; //___added variable
var osc = audioContext.createOscillator();
osc.type = "sine";
osc.connect(audioContext.destination);
osc.start(audioContext.currentTime);
```

Replace the `osc.type` assignment with the `waveformType` variable like this:

```
var audioContext = new AudioContext();
var waveformType = "sawtooth"; //___added variable
var osc = audioContext.createOscillator();
osc.type = waveformType; //__Assigned it to our oscillator type
osc.connect(audioContext.destination);
osc.start(audioContext.currentTime);
```

Launch your web browser, and instead of hearing a sine waveform, you should hear a sawtooth waveform.

In this example, the following declarations assign values to variables that represent other waveform types.

```
var audioContext = new AudioContext();
//___ 4 variables that represent oscillator waveforms
var saw = "sawtooth";
var sine = "sine";
var tri = "triangle";
var square = "square";
//___ A variable intended to contain one of these waveforms
var currentWaveform = undefined;
currentWaveform = square;
//_____Start of oscillator
var osc = audioContext.createOscillator();
osc.type = currentWaveform; // Assigned it to our oscillator type
osc.connect(audioContext.destination);
osc.start(audioContext.currentTime);
```

Each of the four new variables contains a string that represents an oscillator waveform type. The `square` variable is assigned to the `currentWaveform` variable in the following line:

```
currentWaveform = square;
```

Notice that no new declaration is required for the `currentWaveform` variable to assign (and replace) whatever was previously assigned to it. The new data on the right side of "=" is assigned to `currentWaveform`. If you launch your web browser, you will hear a square wave play. In programming, being able to overwrite variables in this manner is referred to as *mutability* (*changeability*), and we say that variables are mutable. The opposite of this is called *immutability*.

▎█ console.log()

When programs begin to get big, it can be difficult to know what value is assigned to a variable at any given moment. One way you can find out is by using a built-in feature called `console.log()`.

The way you do this is by typing `console.log()` into your code at the point where you want to check a given variable's assignment. You then place the *variable name* inside the parentheses.

To see what the `currentWaveform` variable has as its assignment, you do this:

```
var audioContext = new AudioContext();
//Added 4 variables that represent oscillator waveforms
var saw = "sawtooth";
var sine = "sine";
var tri = "triangle";
var square = "square";
var currentWaveform = undefined;
```

```
currentWaveform = square;
console.log(currentWaveform); //___ square
//_____Start of oscillator
var osc = audioContext.createOscillator();
osc.type = currentWaveform; // Assigned it to our oscillator type
osc.connect(audioContext.destination);
osc.start(audioContext.currentTime);
```

Launch Chrome, open the developer tools and click the console tab; you will see the output of our `console.log()`.

One thing to remember is that because variables can have different values at different times, the output of `console.log()` depends on where it is placed in the program. If you modify the last example and place `console.log()` immediately after the `currentWaveform` variable, which has `undefined` assigned to it, then `undefined` is output to the log.

```
//_____A variable intended to contain one of these waveforms
var currentWaveform = undefined;
console.log(currentWaveform); //_____results in "undefined"
currentWaveform = square;
```

So far we've mentioned three of the six data types in JavaScript. The first was `string`, the second was `undefined`, and the last was `null`.

Before we go further, let's explore the string data type a bit more in depth.

▮ String

As we already discovered, strings are denoted by quotation marks. The variable below is a string:

```
var oscillator = "square";
```

You can manipulate strings in different ways. One of the most common is by combining multiple strings into one string. This is called *concatenation*, and it works by using the plus sign (+) like this:

```
var oscillator = "saw" + "tooth";
console.log(oscillator); // sawtooth
```

Here is another example of concatenating two variables and storing them in a new variable.

```
var phrase = "This sound is an ";
var soundType = "oscillator";
var sentence = phrase + soundType;
console.log(sentence); // "This sound is an oscillator".
```

Notice that strings can contain white space.

This is a perfectly valid string, even though it contains a lot of white-space characters:

```
var myFavoriteSynthCompany = "My favorite synth company is Moog";
```

If you want to get the number of characters in a string, you can use what is called the *length property* like this:

```
console.log(myFavoriteSynthCompany.length); // 33
```

The output of the `length` property includes the white-space characters of the string.

Built-In String Methods

JavaScript has a series of built-in tools called *methods* that allow you to manipulate data. Some of these methods are specifically designed to manipulate *string* data.

These are called *string methods*.

To see how to use a string method, take a look at the examples of the `toUpperCase()` and `toLowerCase()` methods.

toUpperCase()

This method changes all the characters in a string to uppercase.

```
var oscillator = "sawtooth";
oscillator.toUpperCase(); // SAWTOOTH
```

toLowerCase()

This method changes all the characters in a string to lowercase.

```
var oscillator = "SAWTOOTH";
oscillator.toLowerCase(); // "sawtooth"
```

Some useful string methods are:

charAt()	Returns a character at any given index in a string
replace()	Finds and replaces a group of characters in a string
slice()	Extracts part of a string

You do not need to immediately memorize how each of these methods works, but it's a good idea to know about them. This way, when you do need to implement any of the functionalities they provide, you know which tool to reach for. If you would like to explore more string methods, a good resource is the Mozilla Developer Network at: https://developer.mozilla.org/en-US/docs/Web/JavaScript/Reference/Global_Objects/String.

Let's go through each one of these and explain how to use them.

charAt()

This method gets a character at any given index value within a string. For example, if you have the string "oscillator-1" and want to know what the second letter of this string is without actually looking at it, you can do this:

```
var sound = "oscillator";
console.log(sound.charAt(1)); // "s"
```

Now you might be wondering why `charAt(1)` returns "s" and not "o". The reason is that the count begins at zero. So, to get the first letter do this:

```
console.log(sound.charAt(0)); // "o"
```

When an index list begins with zero, it is called a *zero-based index*.

replace()

This method finds a group of characters in a string and replaces them with another string. If you want to replace an entire word, you can do it like this:

```
var myFavoriteSynthCompany = "My favorite synth company is
   Moog. Moog is great!";
var myNewFavoriteSynthCompany = myFavoriteSynthCompany.
   replace("Moog","Dave Smith Instruments");
console.log(myNewFavoriteSynthCompany); /*My favorite synth
   company is Dave Smith Instruments. Moog is great!*/
```

As you probably noticed, when using the replace method in this manner it only replaces the first instance of the word you select. To replace all instances of the word, you need to use the following syntax to *globally* replace them in the string.

```
var myFavoriteSynthCompany = "My favorite synth company is
   Moog. Moog is great!";
var myNewFavoriteSynthCompany = myFavoriteSynthCompany.
   replace(/Moog/gi,"Dave Smith Instruments");
console.log(myNewFavoriteSynthCompany); /*My favorite synth company
   is Dave Smith Instruments. Dave Smith Instruments is great!*/
```

The g stands for *global* and the i denotes *case insensitivity*. If you want the string replacement to be case sensitive, you use a g and omit the i. These characters are part of a pattern-matching language for string data called *regular expressions*. Regular expressions are an advanced topic that will not be covered further in this book.

slice()

This method extracts part of a string.

```
var oscillator = "sawtooth";
var sound = oscillator.slice(0,3);
console.log(sound); // saw
```

Like `charAt()`, `slice()` works on a zero-based index. This means the first character is always zero. The slice method takes two values: a beginning index value and an ending index value. When a method takes values, they are called *arguments*. The `charAt()` method takes one argument. The `slice()` method takes two arguments. The slice method's first argument is where the slice starts, and this value is included in the slice. The second value is where the slice ends and is noninclusive. This means all the characters up to, but not including, the second value are included in the slice.

The `length` Property

The `length` property is an additional tool that allows you to get the number of characters in a string. A *property* looks similar to a method but does not include parentheses and does not require arguments to return a value. The character count of the `length` property starts at one, *not* zero.

```
var instrument = "piano";
console.log(instrument.length); // 5
```

If you want to get the last value of a string, you can combine the `length` property with the `charAt()` method. This allows you to retrieve the last character in a string in a manner that doesn't require you to know how long the string is. The code shows an example of this. The reason you subtract 1 from the `length` property is because the `length` property begins counting at one, whereas `charAt()` begins counting at zero. Therefore, you subtract 1 from the `length` property to compensate for the offset.

```
var sound = "oscillator-1";
var oscNumber = sound.charAt(sound.length - 1);
console.log(oscNumber); // 1
```

Numbers

In JavaScript, numbers are a distinct data type. Below is a variable named `frequencyValue`, and it is assigned a number of 200. It is then assigned to the oscillator's pitch. If you place the code below in a new JavaScript file and run it, you will hear an oscillator play at a frequency of 200 Hz. Modify the number value assigned to the `frequencyValue` variable and launch the code to hear the oscillator play at different pitches.

```
var audioContext = new AudioContext();
var frequencyValue = 200; //___Create variable frequencyValue
var waveform = "sawtooth";
var osc = audioContext.createOscillator();
osc.type = waveform;
//_____ assign it to the oscillators pitch
osc.frequency.value = frequencyValue;
osc.connect(audioContext.destination);
osc.start(audioContext.currentTime);
```

How to Determine the Data Type of a Variable

You can discern the difference between data types in variables by using the `typeof` operator.

```
var waveform = "sine";
var polyphony = 16;
```

```
console.log(typeof waveform); // string
console.log(typeof polyphony); // number
```

Unlike strings, numbers do not use quotation marks. In fact, if you did use a number with quotation marks, its data type would *not* be *number*, it would be *string*.

Here's an example:

```
var oscillators = "6";
var polyphony = 6;
console.log(typeof oscillators); // string
console.log(typeof polyphony); // number
```

You can do basic math with numbers using the following symbols. These symbols are called *arithmetic operators*.

+	Addition
–	Subtraction
*	Multiplication
/	Division
%	Modulo

Examples of Arithmetic Operators

```
console.log(5 + 5); // 10
console.log(10 - 5); // 5
console.log(5 * 5); // 25
console.log(25 / 5); // 5
console.log(10 % 9); // 1
```

The last symbol (%) might be new to you, and it is pronounced **moj**-*uh*-loh. The purpose of this symbol is to output the remainder of a division. So, for example:

```
console.log(12 % 9); // This equals 3
```

The precedent rules of algebra also apply. If you wrap a calculation in parentheses, the calculation inside the parentheses is performed first.

Examples of Precedence

```
var oscillator1 = 1000;
var oscillator2 = 100;
var oscillator3 = 20;
var combinedOscillator = oscillator1 +(oscillator2 * oscillator3);
console.log(combinedOscillator); // 3000
```

If you want to do more elaborate calculations, JavaScript has a built-in tool called the *Math object*, which allows you to use a collection of math methods to manipulate numbers.

So, for example, if you want to round a decimal number to its nearest integer, you can use `Math.round()` like this:

```
Math.round(1000.789); // outputs 1001
```

Some useful math object methods are:

`Math.min()`	Finds the smallest number in a collection of numbers
`Math.max()`	Finds the largest number in a collection of numbers
`Math.ceil()`	Rounds a decimal number up to the nearest integer and removes the decimal values
`Math.floor()`	Removes the decimal values of a number, making it an integer
`Math.random()`	Creates a random number between 0 and 1
`Math.abs()`	Returns the absolute value of a number

Let's go over each of these one by one. If you would like to explore more math methods, a good site is the Mozilla Developer Network at: https://developer .mozilla.org/en-US/docs/Web/JavaScript/Reference/Global_Objects/Math.

Math.min() and Math.max()

`Math.min()` finds the smallest number in a collection of numbers, whereas `Math.max()` allows you to find the largest number in a collection of numbers.

```
Math.min(5000, 2000, 80); // 80
Math.max(5000, 2000, 80); // 5000
//_____With variables
var freq_1 = 5000;
var freq_2 = 2000;
var freq_3 = 80;
Math.min(freq_1, freq_2, freq_3); // 80
Math.max(freq_1, freq_2, freq_3); // 5000
```

Math.ceil() and Math.floor()

These two methods turn a decimal number into an integer. `Math.ceil()` rounds up to the next higher integer value if there are any nonzero digits to the right of the decimal, whereas `Math.floor()` keeps the integer value after discarding the digits to the right of the decimal.

```
Math.ceil(3.00333); // 4
Math.floor(3.9999); // 3
```

Math.random()

The random method creates a random number between zero and one.

```
var randomNumber = Math.random();
console.log(randomNumber); // example: 0.019790495047345757
```

You can combine `Math.random()` with `Math.floor()` to create a random number between two values. The expression in the following example creates a random integer between 20 and 20,000.

```
var max = 20000;
var min = 20;
var randomInteger = Math.floor(Math.random() *
  (max - min + 1) + min);
console.log(randomInteger); // Between 20 and 20000
```

Math.abs()

The abs method allows you to get the absolute value of a number.

```
var num = Math.abs(-100);
console.log(num); // 100
```

This is useful for finding the difference between numeric variables of unknown values.

```
var a = 1000;
var b = 5000;
console.log(Math.abs(b - a)); // 4000
```

▌▌ Number-to-String Conversion

If you want to convert between numbers and numeric strings, you can use the following techniques.

To convert a string to a number, place the plus symbol (+) before the string like this:

```
var numericString = "120";
var num = +numericString; // plus symbol
console.log(num); // 120
console.log(typeof num); // number
```

If you want to convert a number to a numeric string, concatenate the number with an empty string like this:

```
var num = 80;
var numericString = num + "";
console.log(numericString); // 80
console.log(typeof numericString); // string
```

If you attempt to do a math operation using nonnumeric values, sometimes you will receive a returned value of NaN. This stands for *not a number*. Here is an example of attempting to add two values in which one value is a number and the other is not.

```
var osc1 = undefined;
var osc2 = 200;
console.log(osc1 + osc2); // NaN
```

▌▌ Arrays

Arrays are a construct that holds multiple pieces of data. You can think of them as variables that hold more than one item. Arrays are expressed using brackets, where each item is separated by a comma. Each item in the array is designated an index number with the first item starting at zero.

```
var waveforms = [ ]; // empty array
var waveforms = ["square", "sawtooth", "triangle", "sine"]; //
  array with some data
```

If you want to access any of these data, you can use the following notation:

```
waveforms[0]; // square
waveforms[1]; // sawtooth
waveforms[2]; // triangle
waveforms[3]; // sine
waveforms[4]; // undefined (no data)
```

If you want to know how many items are inside an array, use the `length` property like this:

```
var waveforms = ["square", "sawtooth", "triangle", "sine"];
waveforms.length; // 4
```

Arrays come with built-in methods that you can use to manipulate the data in them. A full list of these are available at the Mozilla Developer Network at this URL: https://developer.mozilla.org/en-US/docs/Web/JavaScript/Reference/Global_Objects/Array. We are only going to go over a handful of these and they are:

push()	Adds additional items to the end of an array
pop()	Removes a single item from the end of an array
shift()	Removes a single item from the beginning of an array
unshift()	Adds additional items to the beginning of an array
concat()	Concatenates arrays together into one array

push()

This method adds items to the end of an array.

```
var synthFrequencies = [5000, 1000, 500];
synthFrequencies.push(100); /*This places a new item at the end of
  the array*/
console.log(synthFrequencies); // [5000, 1000, 500, 100]
```

You can use the push method to add multiple items at once.

```
var synthFrequencies = [5000, 1000, 500];
synthFrequencies.push(100, 50, 30);
console.log(synthFrequencies); // [5000, 1000, 500, 100, 50, 30]
```

pop()

This method removes a single item at the end of an array.

```
var synthFrequencies = [5000, 1000, 500];
synthFrequencies.pop();
console.log(synthFrequencies); // [5000, 1000]
```

If you want to capture the last item you removed from an array in a variable, do this:

```
var synthFrequencies = [5000, 1000, 500];
var lastItem = synthFrequencies.pop();
console.log(lastItem); // 500
```

shift()

This method removes an item from the beginning of an array.

```
var synthFrequencies = [5000, 1000, 500];
synthFrequencies.shift();
console.log(synthFrequencies); // [1000, 500]
```

If you want to capture the first item you removed from an array in a variable, do this:

```
var synthFrequencies = [5000, 1000, 500];
var firstItem = synthFrequencies.shift();
console.log(firstItem); // 5000
```

unshift()

This method adds new items to the beginning of an array.

```
var synthFrequencies = [5000, 1000, 500];
synthFrequencies.unshift(7500, 6000);
console.log(synthFrequencies); // [7500, 6000, 5000, 1000, 500]
```

concat()

This method merges multiple arrays together into one array.

```
var drumMachines = ["MPC", "Machine", "TR 808"];
var keyboards = ["Juno", "ARP", "Jupiter"];
var percussion = ["vibraphone", "bongos"];
var stringed = ["guitar", "bass", "harp"];
var instruments = drumMachines.concat(keyboards, percussion,
  stringed);
console.log(instruments); /* ['MPC','Machine','TR 808','Juno','ARP',
  'Jupiter','vibraphone','bongos','guitar','bass','harp'] */
```

▮ Summary

In this chapter, you learned about variables, comments, numbers, strings, and arrays. In the next chapter, you will learn about various assignment and logical operators.

3 Operators

You learned about the basic assignment operator (=) and some of the arithmetic operators in the previous chapter. In this chapter, we are going to explore other assignment operators, as well as comparison operators, that allow you to determine the relationship between variables and values, such as whether they have the same value. We will also explore the Boolean data type, which has either a true or a false value that can be assigned to variables or is the result of a comparison operation.

▮▮ What Are Operators?

Operators represent actions that you use to change the value of a variable, or compare values or variables. The word *operand* is used to describe a value being used in an operation involving operators. So in the following example, the operands are 300 and 400. The output of the comparison is said to be what the expression evaluates to. In the following example, the operation evaluates to false.

```
300 == 400 /*The values here (300 and 400) are called operands,
  and the output evaluates to false.*/
```

Operators fall into arithmetic, assignment, or logical categories. The arithmetic operators that we covered in the previous chapter are used with numbers.

The assignment operators are used to assign values to variables. The logical operators are used to compare two values and return a `true` or `false` value based on the result of the comparison.

Assignment Operators

Assignment operators are used to assign data to variables. Here is a list of assignment operators:

Assignment Operator	Name
=	Assignment
+=	Addition assignment
-=	Subtraction assignment
*=	Multiplication assignment
/=	Division assignment
%=	Modulo assignment

Assignment

This operator assigns a value to a variable.

```
var osc = 100;
```

With assignment operators, you can also assign variables to other variables.

```
var osc1 = 100;
var osc2 = osc1;
console.log(osc2); // 100
```

Addition Assignment

This operator increments a numeric variable or appends a string to a variable. In the following example, an oscillator is assigned a value of 100 and then incremented by 100 to give it a value of 200.

```
var osc = 100;
osc += 100;
console.log(osc); // 200
```

To demonstrate the use of the addition assignment operator, the following code sets an ever-increasing frequency change to an oscillator and you can listen to the effect. A method called `setInterval()` is defined, although the specifics of `setInterval()` are not important at this time. What *is* important is understanding that the addition assignment operator is incrementing the frequency value by 100 every 0.5 seconds when `setInterval()` is called.

```
var audioContext = new AudioContext();
var osc = audioContext.createOscillator();
osc.frequency.value = 300;
osc.connect(audioContext.destination);
osc.start(audioContext.currentTime);
```

```
setInterval(function(){
    osc.frequency.value += 100; /*____Increment frequency value by
      100 every 0.5 seconds*/
    console.log(osc.frequency.value); //_____View change
},500); //_____500 milliseconds is 0.5 seconds
```

When you use the addition assignment operator with a string, the string you supply is concatenated with the variable. Here is an example:

```
var keyboards = "";
keyboards += "Korg ";
keyboards += "Yamaha ";
keyboards += "Kurzweil ";
console.log(keyboards); // Korg Yamaha Kurzweil
```

Subtraction Assignment

This operator is used to decrement a numeric variable.

```
var osc = 500;
osc -= 100;
console.log(osc); // 400
```

Multiplication Assignment

This operator multiplies a variable with a value and assigns it to the variable.

```
var osc = 200;
osc *= 2;
osc *= 2;
console.log(osc); // 800
```

Division Assignment

This operator divides a variable by a value and assigns it to the variable.

```
var osc = 200;
osc /= 2;
osc /= 2;
console.log(osc); // 50
```

Modulo Assignment

This operator divides a variable by a value and assigns the *remainder* of that division to the variable.

```
var osc = 200;
osc %= 150;
console.log(osc); // 50
```

The Boolean Data Type

The Boolean data type is either true or false. This is conveyed by the word-form values true and false. Booleans are important because you can use them to program on or off (true or false) values into the code. So, for example, you could use them as a value that toggles an oscillator on or off. Assigning a Boolean value to a variable in JavaScript looks like this:

```
var oscillatorIsOn = true; // true
oscillatorIsOn = false; // changed to false
```

Boolean values can also be the result of the comparison operators described below or used in conditionals statements, which we will cover in the next chapter.

Comparison Operators

Comparison operators are used to compare two variables or values. They output a `true` or `false` value depending on whether the variables or values are similar or different from one another in some way. The similarity or difference being tested for is dependent on the operator used. So, for example, if you test whether two values are the same using the strict equality operator (===) and they are not the same, the resulting value is `false`. There are eight comparison operators.

Comparison Operator	Name
==	Equality operator
===	Strict equality operator
>	Greater than
<	Less than
>=	Greater than or equal to
<=	Less than or equal to
!=	Not equal to
!==	Strict not equal to

Equality Operator

This operator checks whether the left operand is equal to the right operand. It then returns a Boolean value to represent the outcome of the comparison.

```
200 == 200; // true
"200hz" == "200hz"; // true
var osc1 = "200hz";
var osc2 = "200hz";
console.log(osc1 == osc2); // true
```

The equality operator can be a bit tricky because it attempts to do a data type coercion before comparing operands. Data type coercion occurs when the code interpreter (in our case the web browser) attempts to convert one data type into another. In the following example, we compare a number and a numeric string. JavaScript tries to convert the string to a number before doing the comparison. If the string is a numeric string, the conversion is successful, and the comparison is performed. In this case, the result of the comparison is the Boolean value true because the numeric string "200" is successfully converted to the value 200, which matches the value of osc1.

```
var osc1 = 200;
var osc2 = "200";
console.log(osc1 == osc2); // true
```

If a nonnumeric string is compared against a number, the result is always false.

```
200 == "oscillator" // false
```

Strict Equality Operator

To protect against the confusion of type coercion using the equality operator, you can use the strict equality operator. This operator does *not* do data type coercion. This means that, if *any* numeric string is compared against a number, the result is always false. For newer JavaScript programmers, we suggest that you always use this operator. Restricting yourself to this operator helps to mitigate problems involving coercion before they start.

```
//_____Examples
900 === 900 // true
var osc1 = 200;
var osc2 = "200";
console.log(osc1 === osc2); // false
```

Greater Than and Less Than Operators

These operators produce a Boolean result that is based on whether the left operand is less than or greater than the right operand.

```
100 < 200 // true
300 < 200 // false
300 > 200 // true
300 > 500 // false
```

The greater than and less than operators do data type coercion as shown in this example:

```
600 > "500" // true
600 < "500" // false
```

Greater Than or Equal to Operator

This operator returns a Boolean value of true if the first operand is greater than or equal to the second operand.

```
var osc1 = 300;
var osc2 = 500;
var osc3 = 300;
osc3 >= osc1 // true
osc2 >= osc1 // true
osc1 >= osc2 // false
```

The greater than or equal to operator does data type coercion as shown in this example:

```
300 >= "300" // true
```

Less Than or Equal to Operator

This operator returns a Boolean value of true if the left operand is less than or equal to the right operand.

```
300 <= 300 // true
300 <= 500 // true
300 <= 200 // false
```

The less than or equal to operator does data type coercion as shown in these examples:

```
300 <= "300" // true
300 <= "500" // true
300 <= "200" // false
```

Not Equal to Operator

This operator is a combination of the NOT symbol and the equal sign. The NOT symbol is expressed as an exclamation mark and is sometimes referred to as the *bang* operator. When NOT is coupled with an equal sign to produce the not equal to operator, it can be used to return a Boolean value that is based on whether two values are not equal to each other. If the two values are *not equal*, the result is true. If the two values are *equal*, the result is false.

```
300 != 200 // true
300 != 300 // false
```

The not equal to operator does data type coercion as shown in this example:

```
"300" != 300 // false
```

Strict Not Equal to Operator

This operator returns a Boolean value that is based on whether two values are not equal to each other. The strict not equal to operator, unlike the not equal to operator, does not do type coercion.

```
"300" !== 300 // true
300 !== 300 // false
```

Logical Operators

Logical operators allow you to check if a collection of statements is true or false and return a Boolean value based on this information.

Logical Operator	Name
&&	AND
||	OR
!	NOT

The Logical AND Operator

The logical AND operator evaluates to `true` only if all the operands are true. The way it works is that first, the value on the right side of the operator is evaluated, and if its value is false, the Boolean value of `false` is returned. In this case, the value on the left side of the operator is never considered!

If the value on the right side of the operator evaluates to true, then and only then does the AND operator check the value on the left side of the operator. If the value on the left side of the operator is false, then the Boolean value `false` is returned. In the case where both the values on the left and right sides of the logical AND operator are true, the Boolean value `true` is returned.

```
true && true // true
true && false // false
false && true // false
false && false // false
```

The Logical OR Operator

This operator returns `true` as long as either of the operands is true.

```
true || true // true
true || false // true
false || true // true
false || false // false
```

The NOT Operator

This operator inverts a Boolean value.

```
!false // true
!true // false
```

Another way to look at this code is that, if a value is not `false`, then it is true, and if its value is not `true`, then it is false.

In JavaScript, there are six values that evaluate to false. They are the following:

```
false
" "
null
undefined
0
NaN
```

All other values evaluate to `true`.

When you specify the NOT operator twice in a row before a variable or an operand, the resultant value is its original Boolean value.

```
!!false // false
!!true // true
!!0 // false
```

```
!!"" // false
!!null // false
!!undefined // false
!!NaN // false
```

▮ Summary

In this chapter, you learned about JavaScript assignment and logical operators, the Boolean data type, and what values evaluate to `false`. In the next chapter, you will learn to leverage these tools using two new concepts: conditionals and loops.

4 Conditional Statements and Loops

Conditional statements and loops are two of the most widely used constructs in programming. Conditional statements allow your program to make choices based on a set of criteria. Loops use repetition, allowing your program to complete many tasks quickly.

▌▌ Conditional Statements

To create programs that do more than basic calculations or print text, they must be able to make decisions. You can program these decisions by using *conditional statements*. Conditional statements check if a value is true or false and then execute a branch of code based on this condition. We are going to go over the following three conditional statements:

- `if`

- `switch`

- `ternary`

The if Statement

The syntax of an if statement consists of the if keyword, a pair of parentheses, and two curly braces. This is what an empty if statement looks like:

```
if(){
}
```

To use an if statement, you place a value or condition inside the parentheses and some code to execute inside the curly braces. If the condition inside the parentheses evaluates to true, the code inside the curly braces is executed. If the condition evaluates to false, no action is taken and the code inside the curly braces is skipped. In the following code, an if statement is used to check if an oscillator frequency is set to 80 Hz prior to play start. If it is, the oscillator plays; if it is not, the code inside the curly braces is ignored and the oscillator does not play.

```
//_____BEGIN Setup
var audioContext = new AudioContext();
var osc = audioContext.createOscillator();
osc.type = "sawtooth";
osc.frequency.value = 80;
osc.connect(audioContext.destination);
//_____END Setup
//_____BEGIN Check frequency
if(osc.frequency.value === 80){
  osc.start(audioContext.currentTime);
}
//_____END Check frequency
```

If statements can also have an optional else branch that executes if the initial condition evaluates to false. In the following code, the if statement checks to see if frequency.value is 100 Hz. If this condition is true, the oscillator begins to play. If this condition is false, the else branch executes, assigns frequency.value to 50 Hz, and starts the oscillator playing.

```
//_____BEGIN Setup
var audioContext = new AudioContext();
var osc = audioContext.createOscillator();
osc.type = "sawtooth";
osc.frequency.value = 200;
osc.connect(audioContext.destination);
//_____END Setup
//_____BEGIN Conditional
if(osc.frequency.value === 100){
  //__evaluates to false
  osc.start(audioContext.currentTime);
}else{
  //__So this plays
  osc.frequency.value = 50;
  osc.start(audioContext.currentTime);
}
//_____END Conditional
```

Suppose you want to check for more than two conditions and do something different for each one, you can do this by creating an `if` statement with multiple `else if` branches in sequence. The final `else` statement catches all conditions that were not met along the way. An empty example looks like this:

```
if(){

}else if(){

}else{

}
```

In the following working example, the code executes and checks to see if osc.type is set to "sine". If this condition evaluates to false, the `else if` branch runs and checks if the oscillator type is set to "sawtooth". This evaluates to true, and the oscillator starts playing. If osc.type is not set to "sine" or "sawtooth" (in other words, if both conditions evaluated to false), then the result is execution of `console.log()`, which outputs "no condition met."

```
var audioContext = new AudioContext();
var osc = audioContext.createOscillator();
osc.type = "sawtooth";
osc.connect(audioContext.destination);
if(osc.type === "sine"){
  osc.start(audioContext.currentTime);
}else if(osc.type === "sawtooth"){
  osc.frequency.value = 50;
  osc.start(audioContext.currentTime);
}else{
  console.log("no condition met");
}
```

The `switch` Statement

If you catch yourself writing an `if` statement with a lot of `else if` branches, you should consider using a `switch` statement. A `switch` statement allows you to check if a variable has a particular value assigned to it and then runs a block of code that begins where that value is defined. The following code is an example of an empty `switch` statement. The expression in parentheses determines a value. The `case` statements define values that you want to catch and then run some code. Each case statement is terminated by a `break` statement because otherwise the code following the `break` statement is run. At the end of the `switch` statement, you can define the optional `default` keyword that specifies the code to run if none of the other `case` statements evaluate to true (the value is not one that you expected).

```
switch(expression){
  case "value1": //__if true
  //_____then do something
  break;
```

```
  case "value2": //__if true
  //_____then do something
  break;
  default: //____if all other cases are false
  //_____then do this
}
```

The following code is an example of a `switch` statement that checks the value of an oscillator type and sets its frequency value based on its being a sine, sawtooth, or square wave. If the oscillator is not one of these types, the default branch executes and sets `osc.frequency.value` to 200.

```
//_____BEGIN Setup
var audioContext = new AudioContext();
var osc = audioContext.createOscillator();
osc.type = "sawtooth";
osc.connect(audioContext.destination);
//_____END Setup
//_____BEGIN Switch statement
switch(osc.type) {
  case "sawtooth":
    osc.frequency.value = 50;
    osc.start(audioContext.currentTime)
  break;
  case "sine":
    osc.frequency.value = 100;
    osc.start(audioContext.currentTime);
  break;
  case "square":
    osc.frequency.value = 150;
    osc.start(audioContext.currentTime);
  break;
  default:
    osc.frequency.value = 200;
    osc.start(audioContext.currentTime);

}
//_____END Switch statement
```

Ternary Operator

If you are writing a conditional statement that contains a single comparison clause (it returns only one of two conditions), then you can use a ternary operator. The ternary operator has three parts: an expression and two executed statements. The first part is an expression that is tested for true or false and is separated from the executed code by a question mark. If the expression evaluates to true, the code to the left of the colon is run. If the expression evaluates to false, the code to the right of the colon is run. The syntax of the ternary operator looks like this:

```
/*
expression ? if true run this code : if false run this code
*/
```

The following code is an example of the ternary operator in action. This code checks if the oscillator type is set to "sawtooth". If it is, the frequency is set to 50; otherwise, it is set to 500.

```
//_____BEGIN setup
var audioContext = new AudioContext();
var osc = audioContext.createOscillator();
osc.type = "sine";
osc.connect(audioContext.destination);
osc.start(audioContext.currentTime);
//_____END setup
//_____BEGIN Ternary example
osc.type === "sawtooth" ? osc.frequency.value = 50 : osc.frequency.
  value = 500;
//_____END Ternary example
```

▌ Loops

Computers are very good at doing lots of simple tasks very fast. One of the tools available to leverage this capability is *loops*. Loops allow you to repeat a task until a condition or set of conditions are met. We will cover the following types of loops:

- for

- while

for Loops

The following code is an example of a for loop that counts to 16 and outputs each loop number to the console. The text that follows explains the keywords and what each component of the for loop does.

```
for(var i = 0; i <=16; i+=1) {
   console.log(i);
}
```

A for loop consists of the for keyword and opening and closing parentheses. Inside the parentheses are three parts separated by semicolons. The first part is the initialization variable, and in this case it is set to zero.

```
for(var i = 0; i <=16; i+=1) {
   console.log(i);
}
```

The next part is the conditional statement, which is used to determine a condition to check upon each iteration of the loop. As long as this condition is true, the loop will iterate (run another time). In the following example, the condition tells the for loop to continue iterating as long as the value of the variable i is less than or equal to 16.

```
for(var i = 0; i <=16; i+=1) {
   console.log(i);
}
```

The next part is used to increment the initialization variable. On each loop, the variable i is incremented by one and eventually reaches 17 and stops looping.

```
for(var i = 0; i <=16; i+=1){
  console.log(i);
}
```

The last part of a for loop is the code block that is defined by the opening and closing curly braces. Any code that is written in between these curly braces gets repeated for each loop iteration.

```
for(var i = 0; i <=16; i+=1){
  console.log(i); // code here gets repeated for each loop
}
```

When for loops are run, they are very fast. Below is a script that uses an additional helper function to pause each iteration of a for loop. The loop modifies the frequency of a playing oscillator on each iteration. The helper function pauses the loop (which is its only function), so you can *hear* each change.

```
/*_____BEGIN Helper function.
Ignore this code it is simply being used to pause the for loop */
function sleep(milliseconds) {
  var start = new Date().getTime();
  for (var i = 0; i < 1e7; i++) {
    if ((new Date().getTime() - start) > milliseconds){
      break;
    }
  }
}
//_____END Helper function
//_____BEGIN Web Audio API setup
var audioContext = new AudioContext();
var osc = audioContext.createOscillator();
osc.type = "sawtooth";
osc.frequency.value = 30;
osc.connect(audioContext.destination);
osc.start(audioContext.currentTime);

//_____END Web Audio API setup
//_____BEGIN audible for-loop example
for(var i =0 ; i < 10; i+=1){
  osc.frequency.value +=100;
  sleep(500);
}
//_____END audible for-loop example
```

Using for Loops with Arrays

It is common to use loops to modify and extract data from arrays. The following code has an empty array and a for loop. The for loop iterates four times, and on each iteration, the string "synth" is concatenated with the i variable and is pushed to the synths array. The result is the creation of four entries in the `synths` array, each consisting of the word "synth" followed by a dash and a number.

```
var synths = [];
for (var i = 1; i <= 4; i += 1) {
  synths.push("synth-" + i);
}
console.log(synths); //[ 'synth-1', 'synth-2', 'synth-3', 'synth-4' ]
```

If you want to modify each value in an existing array, you can do so by looping through the array and modifying the value at each iteration. To do this, set the conditional statement termination value to the length of the array. In the following code, this is done with `synths.length`. You can then access the individual values of the array within the loop by placing the iterator variable inside the brackets next to it.

```
var synths = [ 'synth-1', 'synth-2', 'synth-3', 'synth-4' ];
console.log(synths.length); //__This is 4
for (var i = 0; i < synths.length; i += 1) {
  console.log(synths[i]);
}
```

The following code shows a modification of the previous code where each value in the array has "0hz" appended to it.

```
var synths = ['synth-1', 'synth-2', 'synth-3', 'synth-4'];
for (var i = 0; i < synths.length; i += 1) {
  synths[i] += "0hz";
}
console.log(synths); /*[ 'synth-10hz', 'synth-20hz', 'synth-30hz',
  'synth-40hz']*/
```

while Loops

The `while` loop is useful when you are unsure of how many iterations will be needed to complete a task. A simple example is a live podcast website that allows users to connect and listen while a show is on the air. As a programmer you might not know how long the show will last but you want to continuously check for new user connections for the duration of the show and allow them to listen in. The pseudocode for this example might look something like this:

```
var onAir = true;
while(onAir){
  // check for new visitors and connect them
}
```

The `while` loop consist of the `while` keyword, opening and closing parentheses, and opening and closing curly braces. A conditional statement is placed in the parentheses, which allows the loop to iterate as long as the condition remains true. When the condition becomes false, the loop stops. The following example loops as long as the `freq` variable is greater than zero. At each iteration, the `freq` variable decrements until it is zero and the loop terminates.

```
var freq = 7000;
while (freq > 0) {
  console.log(freq);
  freq -= 100;
}
```

When to Use for Loops and When to Use while Loops

The rule of thumb for deciding whether to use a `for` or `while` loop is that a `for` loop is typically used when you know the number of iterations that are needed to complete the loop, and a `while` loop is used when you don't know how many iterations are needed to complete the loop.

▮▮ Summary

In this chapter, you have learned how to incorporate decision-making into your programs using conditional statements. You have also learned how to use loops to accomplish tasks quickly and how loops can be leveraged when working with arrays. In the next chapter, you will learn how to incorporate functions into your programs.

5 Functions

In this chapter, you will learn about functions, various ways to work with functions, and variable scope. Functions allow you to write code in a way that avoids repetition. They also allow you to encapsulate your code and perform a specific task based on a set of inputs. Scope pertains to the context in which variables are declared. JavaScript handles variables differently depending on their scope, and you will learn how to use variables in functions when writing programs.

▌ Functions—A Simple Example

To explain functions, let's look at the design of an audio effects module. Imagine a simple hardware audio effects box equipped with a single input channel and a single output channel. Now imagine this effects box *changes* the original input in some way depending on a collection of user-defined settings. In this design, the output of the effects box is the result of the input signal *combined* with the user settings that produce some change in the original signal.

The following example shows how you might code the effects box example for a fixed selection. The effectsBox function takes an input, multiplies that input by two, and returns the result.

```
function effectsBox(input) {
  return input * 2;
}
console.log(effectsBox(120)); // Output 240
```

The following example shows how you can multiply the input by a value selected by the user, which is coded in the form of a parameter called multiplier.

```
function effectsBox(input, multiplier) {
  return input * multiplier;
}
console.log(effectsBox(120, 2)); // Output 240
```

Parts of a Function

To create a function, you start by typing the function keyword followed by a function name. Immediately following the function name, you place opening and closing parentheses, and then immediately after these you place opening and closing curly braces.

```
function add(){
  // function body
}
```

You can give the function placeholders for input values called *parameters*, which you place inside the parentheses and separate by commas.

```
function add(a, b){

}
```

The final part of a function is an optional return statement that outputs a value when the function completes.

```
function add(a, b){
  return a + b;
}
```

To run the function (also called *invoking* the function), you type the function name followed by an opening parenthesis. If the function has parameters, you enter values for these, which in the context of invoking the function are called *arguments*. You end the function with a closing parenthesis.

```
add(2, 5); // 7
```

If you invoke the function with arguments not defined by the function, no error is returned and the system ignores the additional arguments.

```
add(2, 5, 999); //__The third argument is ignored and output is 7
```

Function Expressions

As an alternative to using function declaration syntax, you can write your functions using expression syntax, where you assign the function to a variable like this:

```
var add = function (a,b){
  return a + b;
};
add(2,3); // 5
```

The function expression syntax emphasizes an important aspect of JavaScript functions: they can be treated like data and passed around between variables. Here's an example of the previous code with a variable named container that stores the result of running the add function with arguments 2 and 3:

```
var add = function (a, b) {
  return a + b;
};
var container = add(2, 3);
console.log(container); // 5
```

Abstracting Oscillator Playback

The following function playOsc plays an oscillator and has two arguments. The first, oscType, determines the oscillator waveform type, which for the Web Audio API supports sine, sawtooth, triangle, and square in the form of a string. The second argument is the frequency value in hertz. Because the code necessary to generate the oscillator is encapsulated in a function, you can now invoke the function by writing only one line of code each time you create an oscillator.

This means you avoid the repetition of writing out all of the oscillator creation code every time you create the oscillator.

```
var audioContext = new AudioContext(); //___Initializes web audio api

function playOsc(oscType, freq) {
  var osc = audioContext.createOscillator();
  osc.type = oscType;
  osc.frequency.value = freq; //____freq is a parameter
  osc.connect(audioContext.destination);
  osc.start(audioContext.currentTime);
}

playOsc("sine", 330); //____Plays oscillator at 330hz

/*____We can play multiple oscillators at once using only
  one line of code each time! Adding another sine at 340 will
  create a pulsating effect*/

playOsc("sine", 340);
```

A Working Effects Box Example

The following code demonstrates a simplified working example of how an effects box might look when written as a function. The example consists of three functions. The first two functions generate oscillators. The third function is the actual effectsBox() function that accepts an oscillator and a filter value as inputs, and then applies the filter to the oscillator.

```
var audioContext = new AudioContext();
//_____BEGIN Custom sound
function customSound(filterVal) {
  var osc_1 = audioContext.createOscillator();
  var osc_2 = audioContext.createOscillator();
  var filter = audioContext.createBiquadFilter();
  filter.type = "lowpass";
  osc_1.type = "sawtooth";
  osc_1.frequency.value = 300;
  osc_2.type = "sawtooth";
  osc_2.frequency.value = 402;
  filter.frequency.value = filterVal || filter.frequency.value;
  osc_1.connect(filter);
  osc_2.connect(filter);
  filter.connect(audioContext.destination);
  osc_1.start(audioContext.currentTime);
  osc_2.start(audioContext.currentTime);
}
//_____END Custom sound

//_____BEGIN square wave
function square(filterVal) {
  var osc = audioContext.createOscillator();
  var filter = audioContext.createBiquadFilter();
  filter.type = "lowpass";
  osc.type = "square";
  osc.frequency.value = 100;
```

```
      filter.frequency.value = filterVal || filter.frequency.value;
      osc.connect(filter);
      filter.connect(audioContext.destination);
      osc.start(audioContext.currentTime);
    }

    //_____END square wave

    //_____BEGIN effectsBox

    function effectsBox(sourceInput, filterParam) {
      sourceInput(filterParam);
    }
    //_____END effectsBox
    effectsBox(customSound, 80); // Example
```

The Arguments Object

JavaScript contains an array-like object that allows you to access the arguments of a function in the form of a zero-based list. This pseudo-array does not have access to any of the methods of a conventional array *except* the length property. The following code outputs the argument values by specifying the arguments object in console.log().

```
function playOsc(oscType, freq){
  console.log(arguments[0]);
  console.log(arguments[1]);
}
playOsc("sine", 200); // sine 200
```

You can use the arguments object to create default values for function arguments. The following code checks to see if an argument is undefined, and if it is, sets its value to "sawtooth."

```
function playOsc(oscType) {
  //_____Set default of oscType to sawtooth
  if (arguments[0] === undefined) {
    oscType = "sawtooth";
  }
  return oscType;
}
console.log(playOsc()); //___sawtooth
console.log(playOsc("sine")); //___sine
```

The arguments object can be combined with the length property and a conditional statement to ensure that an error is given if any arguments are left empty. To create your own error statement, you use the throw keyword. In the following code, the conditional statement checks to see if the number of arguments is *not* two, and if the conditional evaluates to true, then an error is given (or *thrown*) to indicate this result.

```
function playOsc(oscType,freq){
  if(arguments.length !==2){
    throw "Error! This function takes two arguments"
  }
```

```
}
playOsc("sine"); //___Error! This function takes two arguments
```

You can add another check to ensure that the correct data types are being entered like this:

```
function playOsc(oscType, freq) {
  if (arguments.length !== 2) {
    throw "Error! This function takes two arguments";
  }
  //_____Check for correct argument data types
  if (typeof oscType !== "string" || typeof freq !== "number") {
    throw "Please enter the correct argument types";
  }
}
playOsc(100, true); //___Please enter the correct argument types
```

You can also use the `arguments` object to limit an argument to a list of specific values. The following function takes a single argument that is intended to be one of the four waveform types. If the argument is not one of these four values, an error is thrown. When the function is invoked, the code loops through an array of the four waveform types. If any of the waveform types matches the argument value, a variable named `waveformValid` is set to the Boolean value `true`. Then a conditional statement checks the value of `waveformValid`. If it is false, an error is thrown; otherwise, the function runs to completion.

```
function playOsc(oscType){
  var waveforms = ["sawtooth","sine","triange","square"];
  var waveformValid = false;
  for(var i =0; i < waveforms.length; i+=1){
    if(arguments[0] === waveforms[i]){
      waveformValid = true;
    }
  }
  if(waveformValid === false){
    throw "please enter sawtooth, sine, triangle or square
      as an argument"
  }
}
playOsc("fat beats");
/*___Error: Uncaught please enter sawtooth, sine, triangle or
  square as an argument___*/
playOsc("square"); //___works
```

▮ Function Scope

Scope is a concept that defines how one part of a program can access variables in another part of a program. In the ECMAScript 5 version of JavaScript, there are only two forms of scopes: a global scope and function scope (also called a *local* scope). This means that if you declare a variable within a function, it is specific to *that* function and does not conflict with any other variables that have the same name and are defined outside of that function. Functions have access to their own variables and they also have access to any variables in a *higher* scope, which includes the global scope.

In one of our previous examples, we created a function to play an oscillator. Notice that although the `audioContext` variable is not included inside the `playOsc` function, it is still accessible. This is because `audioContext` is defined in a higher scope: the global scope.

```
//____audioContext is global
var audioContext = new AudioContext();
//____ playOsc has access to it
function playOsc(oscType, freq){
   var osc = audioContext.createOscillator();
   osc.type = oscType;
   osc.frequency.value = freq; //____freq is a parameter
   osc.connect(audioContext.destination);
   osc.start(audioContext.currentTime);
}
playOsc("sine", 330);//____Plays oscillator at 330hz
```

You can use function scope to protect variables defined in a function not only from variables defined in a higher scope but from variables defined in other functions. In the following example, there are two functions. One *has* data, and the other *wants* data. The data of the first function is *not* accessible to the other function because it is hidden in a local scope.

```
function iHaveData() {
   var data = "The data";
}
function iWantData() {
   return data;
}
iWantData(); // data is not defined
```

If you declare two variables with the same name and one is globally scoped (or in a higher scope) and the other is locally scoped within a function, the locally scoped variable is referenced when the code in the function is running.

So, for example, in the following code, the `multFreq` function takes a single argument and multiplies it by a value that is assigned to the `multiplier` variable. The globally scoped `multiplier` is not referenced when `mult-Freq()` is running because the function has a locally scoped variable with the same name.

```
var multiplier = 4; /*_____This variable is not referenced by
   multFreq*/
function multFreq(frequency) {
   var multiplier = 2; //____Because this one has the same name
   return frequency * multiplier;
}
console.log(multFreq(200)); // 400
console.log(multiplier); // 4
```

If the locally scoped `multiplier` variable declaration inside the previous function is removed, then during function execution, the code will look outside the function for a variable with the referenced name.

```
var multiplier = 4;
function multFreq(frequency) {
  /*__There is no local multiplier variable so it finds one in the
    scope above it__*/
  return frequency * multiplier;
}
console.log(multFreq(200)); // 800
```

Why You Should Always Declare Your Variables with `var`

In JavaScript, the use of global variables should generally be kept to a minimum. This is because when programs get large, the accumulation of global variables increases the likelihood of naming collisions. Typically, this is not a problem for small applications. However, when programs begin to grow, they will usually incorporate libraries and third-party scripts that depend on some global variables. Accidently overwriting these global variables can cause your program to break.

When you declare a variable from within a function *without* the `var` statement, the variable is referenced from the global scope when the function is invoked. This can have the side effect of overwriting a preexisting global variable with the same name and creating an unexpected name collision. The following code demonstrates how this can happen.

The following example contains a global variable called `multiplier`. There is also a variable called `multiplier` inside of the `multFreq` function that is not declared using the `var` statement. When the function is invoked, the `multiplier` variable references the global `multiplier` variable, changing its value from 4 to 2! This is an example of why you should *always* declare your variables with the `var` statement.

```
var multiplier = 4;
function multFreq(frequency) {
  multiplier = 2; //_____Notice no var declaration!
  return frequency * multiplier;
}
console.log(multFreq(200)); // 400
console.log(multiplier); //____Changed to 2!
```

Variable Hoisting

Whether you declare your variables globally or within a function, you should always declare them at the top of the current scope. The reason for this is a phenomenon called hoisting. To understand hoisting, you must first understand that variable declaration and initialization are two different things. In the following code, a variable is declared using the `var` statement and then it is initialized on the next line.

```
var myData; //_____variable declared
myData = "important data goes here";//__variable initialized
//The following variable is declared and initialized in one line
var playOsc = false;
```

When you declare a variable, the JavaScript interpreter immediately (behind the scenes) decouples the declaration from the initialization and moves the variable declaration to the top of the current scope. The following example demonstrates this. The code on the left shows a function named run that contains a variable named test, which is declared *after* it is initialized. When this function is invoked, JavaScript changes the order and places the declaration at the top of the current scope, in effect making the function look identical to the code on the right. This is why the globally scoped test variable is not overwritten when the function is invoked, even though it appears at first glance that it should be, because the local test variable is not yet declared. Because of hoisting, it is considered best practice to declare your variables at the top of the current scope, *which is where they will be declared anyway.*

```
hoisting_example_1.js
1
2
3  function run(){
4      test = "the data";
5      var test;
6  }
7
8  run();
```

```
hoisting_example_2.js
1
2
3  function run(){
4      var test;
5      test = "the data";
6  }
7
8  run();
```

How Hoisting Affects Functions

In addition to hoisting affecting variables, it also affects functions. And hoisting works differently based on whether the function is written with declaration or expression syntax.

Consider the following function declaration. In this code, the function is invoked before it is declared, yet it still works! This is because behind the scenes, the declaration is hoisted to the top of the scope, which allows you to execute the function even though it is not yet declared.

```
multFreq(200, 2); /*__This still works even though it is invoked
  before it is declared!_*/
function multFreq(input, val) {
  return input * val;
}
```

The following example of the same function written using expression syntax, however, throws an error. This happens because function expressions are treated like variables, with the declaration being hoisted to the top. Remember that the initialization of the variable still happens where the variable is initialized in the code. In this case, the function is run before the initialization that defines the function occurs. The lesson here is that when you use function expressions, you must declare functions before you invoke them. This is good practice with all your functions as it makes your code less confusing and more readable.

```
multFreq(200, 2); //___ error! "multFreq is not a function".
var multFreq = function(input, val) {
  return input * val
}
```

▌ Anonymous Functions

Anonymous functions are functions that do not have a name. Technically, the function in the following code is an anonymous function because the variable it is assigned to is not the function name. It is the container name for an anonymous function.

```
var multFreq = function(input, val) {
  return input * val;
}
```

To give this function a name, you do it like this:

```
var multFreq = function nameGoesHere(input, val) {
  return input * val;
}
```

Note, however, that to invoke the function, you use the variable name that it is assigned to.

```
multFreq(100,2); // 200
```

In JavaScript, it is possible to create a function that is invoked immediately after it is declared. This type of function is called an *immediately invoked function expression* or IIFE (pronounced "iffy"). This method is useful if you want to briefly encapsulate and run a block of code only once. The syntax looks like this:

```
//_____BEGIN IIFE
(function run() {
  return "data";
}());
//_____END IIFE
```

To view the output, you can wrap it in `console.log()`.

```
console.log(
//_____BEGIN IIFE
(function run() {
  return "data";
}());
//_____END IIFE
);
```

The first thing to notice is that the function is wrapped in parentheses. This is optional, but is considered best practice because it helps differentiate the construct syntactically from non-IIFE functions.

```
(function run() {
  return "data";
}());
```

The next thing to notice is the parentheses toward the end of the function before the closing, encapsulating parenthesis. This syntax is what invokes the function.

```
(function run() {
  return "data";
}());
```

To add parameters and arguments, you put parameters in the first set of parentheses and aruguments in the second set of parentheses.

```
(function add(a, b) { //_____ parameters
  return a + b;
}(2, 3)); //_____arguments
```

▎▎ Closures

One of the most difficult aspects of the JavaScript language for new programmers to grasp is closures. Understanding closures will ultimately allow you to write cleaner code while giving you a powerful tool to solve a host of problems you will inevitably run into. Understanding the concept of closure can be a bit difficult at first. But in the long term, the benefits are worth the time investment.

What Is a Closure?

A closure is an inner function that has access to the scope of its outer environment even after that outer environment has returned. To understand what this means, you must first solidify your understanding of scope. The following example demonstrates how a function has access to its local scope, the global scope, and its local arguments.

```
var globalVariable = "global variable";
function doSomething(argInput) {
  var localVariable = "local variable";
  console.log(argInput);
  console.log(globalVariable);
  console.log(localVariable);
}

doSomething("argument input"); /*_____This outputs: "argument
    input" "global variable" "local variable" because the function
    has access to its own scope and the outer scope.*/
```

If a function is defined inside another function, it too has access to the data of the harboring function, as well as its own locally scoped variables. In the following example, `testScope()` is a harboring function for `innerFunction()`.

```
var globalVariable = "global variable";

function testScope(argInput) {
  var testScopeLocalVariable = "local variable from testScope";
  //____The inner function has access to everything outside of it
  function innerFunction() {
    var localVariable = "local variable from innerFunction";
    console.log(argInput);
    console.log(globalVariable);
    console.log(testScopeLocalVariable);
    console.log(localVariable);
  }

  innerFunction();
}

testScope("argument input");

/*The console logs:
"argument input"
"global variable"
"local variable from testScope"
"local variable from innerFunction"
*/
```

As we mentioned, a closure is an inner function that has access to the scope of its outer environment *even after that outer environment has returned*. The previous examples demonstrated scope access. The following example demonstrates what it means for a function to have scope access even after the outer environment has returned. The outer environment can be either the global environment or another function. The following code includes the `effectsBox` function that contains a single variable named `component`. The effectsBox function returns a function that returns the value of `component`. When the initial `effectsBox` function is invoked, it returns a function declaration named `openEffectsBox` to the outer scope (in this case the global scope). This `openEffectsBox` function declaration is then assigned to a variable called `getComponent`, which is then invoked and returns the string "Pulled out component."

The important thing to realize here is that a closure (the inner function) can return data (such as the `component` variable) from its containing environment [in this case `effectsBox()`] even after that outer environment [effectsBox()] has returned.

```
function effectsBox() {
  var component = "Pulled out component";
  return function openEffectsBox() {
    return component;
  };
}
```

```
var getComponent = effectsBox(); /*___stores "openEffectsBox"
   function in a variable.*/
console.log(getComponent()); // "Pulled out component"
```

The previous example can be modified to demonstrate how *state can be modified and retained* using the closure. In this code, there is an additional counter variable that increments each time the inner openEffectsBox function is invoked. Since closures allow access to the scope of a containing function even after that containing function has returned, the returned function can continue to increment the counter variable and have access to its state.

```
function effectsBox() {
   var counter = 0;
   var component = "Pulled out component";
   return function openEffectsBox() {
      return component + " " + (counter += 1);
   };
}
var getComponent = effectsBox(); //___stores "openEffectsBox"
   function in a variable.

getComponent(); // "Pulled out component 1"
getComponent(); // "Pulled out component 2"
getComponent(); // "Pulled out component 3"
getComponent(); // "Pulled out component 4"
```

Here is an example of a function designed to play an oscillator by returning an inner function that remembers the outer environment's state. This example shows how the inner function accesses the function arguments of the outer function even after the outer function returns. The playOsc function takes parameter type, whereas the inner function it returns takes parameter freq. The outer function is invoked with the argument "sine"; thereafter, the inner function is invoked with a frequency value. The result is a sine wave that plays at a set frequency value of 140 Hz.

```
var audioContext = new AudioContext();

function playOsc(type) {

   return function(freq) {
      var osc = audioContext.createOscillator();
      osc.type = type;
      osc.frequency.value = freq;
      osc.connect(audioContext.destination);
      osc.start(audioContext.currentTime);
   };
}
var sinewave = playOsc("sine");
sinewave(140); //_____Plays sine wave at 140 hz
```

Closure is an advanced concept that can be used to protect a portion of a program from the global scope, retain state, and organize your code. Its specific use cases will gradually become more apparent as your skill as a programmer develops. For now, it is important to grasp what a closure is.

▮ Callback Functions

A `callback` is a function that is used as an argument to another function. The following example demonstrates addition of two numbers using a callback.

```
function doMath(callback) {
  return callback();
}

function addTwoNumbers() {
  return 2 + 2;
}
doMath(addTwoNumbers); // 4
```

When working with callbacks, you will often see function invocations where the callback declaration is placed directly in a function argument.

```
function doStuff(callback) {
  return callback();
}

doStuff(function() { // ___Callback declaration is used directly
  return //___data
});
```

The following function is an example of using a callback to make a function more flexible. The `calculateFrequencies` function is designed to take three arguments. The first two are numbers and the third is a callback that manipulates the other arguments. If the user does not use a callback, then the function defaults to multiplying the two arguments together.

```
function calculateFrequencies(a, b, callback) {
  if (callback === undefined) {
    return a * b;
  } else {
    return callback(a, b);
  }
}
function diff(a, b) {
  return Math.abs(a - b);
}

console.log(calculateFrequencies(200, 2));// 400___Multiplies numbers
console.log(calculateFrequencies(1000, 4000, diff));/*3000___uses
  custom callback to find the difference*/
```

The previous example demonstrates how passing a callback to a function provides the *action* taken by the callback, whereas passing nonfunction values provides *data* input.

Working with JavaScript's Built-In Callback Functions

Learning to design your own functions that use callbacks is an advanced topic. As a beginner, the more important thing for you to know is how to use preexisting methods that have been designed to use callbacks. The following are two examples of built-in JavaScript methods that use callbacks to help you work with arrays.

Array Method	Description
filter()	Compares each element in an array to a conditional statement and returns a new array of elements that meet the condition
map()	Calls a function on each element in an array and returns a new array with the mapped value of each element in the input array

filter()

The `filter` method compares each element in an array to a conditional statement and returns a new array of only those elements that meet the filter condition. The following example uses `filter()` to loop through an array of frequency values to create a new array of values greater than or equal to 1000.

```
var freq1 = 1200,
    freq2 = 570,
    freq3 = 100,
    freq4 = 1500;

var frequencyList = [freq1, freq2, freq3, freq4];

var filteredFrequencies = frequencyList.filter(function(value) {
  return value >= 1000;
});

console.log(filteredFrequencies); //___ [1200,1300]
```

map()

The map function calls a function on each element in an array and returns a new array that contains the mapped data for each element in the input array.

The following example uses `map()` to add 100 to each value in an array and return a new array named `newFreqs`.

```
var freqs = [100, 200, 300];
var newFreqs = freqs.map(function (val) {
  return val + 100;
});

console.log(newFreqs); //___ [ 200, 300, 400 ]
```

The callback functions of both `map()` and `filter()` take three arguments. In order of their position, these are `value`, `index`, and `array`. The `value` argument is the array value at the current index, the `index` argument is the current index value, and the `array` argument is the array that the callback is being applied to. In the following example, a `map` method is applied to an array and all three arguments are logged to the console.

```
var freqs = [100, 200, 300];
var newFreqs = freqs.map(function(val, index, arr) {
  var message = "current value: " + val + " current index index: "
    + index + " array: " + arr;
  console.log(message);
  return val;
});
/*___This logs the following to the console
current value: 100 current index: 0 array: 100,200,300
current value: 200 current index: 1 array: 100,200,300
current value: 300 current index: 2 array: 100,200,300
*/
```

▌ Recursion

Recursion is an advanced programming topic, and it will only be explored briefly in this chapter.

A recursive function is a function that calls itself. The following is an example of a recursive function.

```
function x(){
  return x()
}
```

If you run the previous code, it will crash your browser. This is because, when a recursive function runs indefinitely, it eventually uses up the resources of your code interpreter (in this case the web browser) and creates an error. To use recursion effectively, you need to set a condition to terminate the recursion. This condition is called the *base case*.

The following example is a recursive function named `loopFromTo` that contains a working base case. `loopFromTo` takes two arguments, and both are numbers. In the function body, a conditional is used to check if the argument named `start` is less than the argument named `end`. As long as this condition is true, `loopFromTo` calls itself and on each iteration increments the `start` argument by one. This continues until the recursion terminates when `start` ceases to be less than `end` and the conditional statement evaluates to false.

```
function loopFromTo(start, end) {
  console.log(start);
  if (start < end) {
    return loopFromTo(start += 1, end)
  }
}

loopFromTo(1, 8) //_____ 1,2,3,4,5,6,7,8
```

Recursive functions can be used in place of looping constructs and are an invaluable tool in many complex algorithms. If recursion seems confusing don't worry, you can program perfectly good applications while you become familiar with it.

▮ Summary

In this chapter, you learned how to create and use functions. In the next chapter, you will expand your understanding of JavaScript to include a concept called object-orientated programming.

6 Objects

So far, we discussed five of JavaScript's six data types. These are string, number, Boolean, undefined, and null. These are called *primitive data types*. Anything that is not a primitive data type is of the *object* data type. In the previous chapter, you learned about functions, which are of the object data type. In this chapter, you will learn how to program using object literals, which are also of the object data type.

JavaScript Data Types

The JavaScript data types are:

- String

- Number

- Boolean

- Undefined

- Null

- Object

The object data type includes functions, arrays, and object literals. Arrays and functions have already been explored, so here is a general definition of object literals: Object literals are a collection of comma-separated key-value pairs that are contained within curly braces.

Note: Developers in the JavaScript world commonly refer to object literals as objects. However, object literals and the object data type are two different things. One way to understand the difference is to recognize that the object data type is a category that contains object literals, functions, and arrays.

In the following code, an object named `obj` is created and the values within curly braces are assigned to it.

```
var obj = {
  key1: "value1",
  key2: "value2"
};
```

A key is similar to a variable, and a value is similar to the data assigned to a variable. The key and value of an object is called a *property* for nonfunctions assigned to a key, or a *method* for functions assigned to a key.

```
var obj = {
  key: "value", //___This is a property
  doSomething: function(){ //___This is a method
  }
};
```

Conceptually, object literals are used to model real-world elements in your code. So, for example, the following object is used to model a music album.

```
//_____This is an object that contains album data
var album = {
  name:"Thriller Funk",
  artist:"James Jackson",
  format:"wave",
  sampleRate:44100
}
```

To access data from an object, you can use dot notation, which looks like this:

```
album.name; // Thriller Funk
album.artist; // James Jackson
album.format; // wave
album.sampleRate; // 44100
```

Alternatively, you can use bracket notation to access values in an object.

```
album["sampleRate"]; // 44100
```

If you use a bracket notation, you must type the key in the form of a string.

```
album["sampleRate"]; //__The key is a string
```

You can use methods to modify or retrieve data from an object. Here is an example of an object that contains a method that returns the name and artist information of an object named *song*.

```
var song = {
  name: "Funky Shuffle",
  artist: "James Jackson",
  format: "wave",
  sampleRate: 44100,
  //_____BEGIN Method
    nameAndArtist: function() {
      return "Name: " + song.name + " | " + "Artist: " + song.artist
    }
  //_____END Method
}
```

You can invoke methods with dot notation and trailing parentheses.

```
//_____BEGIN method invocation
song.nameAndArtist(); // Name: Funky Shuffle| Artist: James Jackson
//_____END method invocation
```

▐ Looping through Objects

To loop through the keys and values of an object, you use a for in loop. You code a for in loop like this:

```
var song = {
  name: "Funky Shuffle",
  artist: "James Jackson",
  format: "wave",
  sampleRate: 44100
}
//_____BEGIN for in loop
for (var prop in song) {
  console.log(prop + ":"); //__Outputs each key
  console.log(song[prop]); //__Outputs each value
}
//_____END for in loop
```

The structure of a for in loop consists of the for keyword followed by a variable that represents the value of each property. In the previous example, this variable was named prop. The variable name is followed by the in keyword and the name of the object you want to loop through.

Often you will want to modify the properties of an object you are looping through while not modifying any of its methods. One way you can do this is by using a conditional statement and the *typeof* operator to act only on property values that are *not* functions. This usage is shown in the following code:

```
var song = {
  name: "Funky Shuffle",
  artist: "James Jackson",
  format: "wave",
  sampleRate: 44100,
  nameAndArtist: function() {
    return "Name: " + song.name + " | " + "Artist: " + song.artist;
  }

};

for (var prop in song) {
  if (typeof song[prop] !== "function") {
    console.log(song[prop]); //___Omits methods
  }
}
```

When to Use Objects Rather Than Arrays

You have probably noticed that objects and arrays are similar because they allow you to organize collections of data. If you are curious about when to use an array rather than an object, the rule of thumb is that if the order of the data matters, you should *always* use an array. The reason for this is that there is nothing in the JavaScript specification that guarantees the order in which key-value pairs of an object are returned in a loop.

How to Check If an Object Has Access to a Particular Property or Method

If you want to check whether a property or method is available to an object, you can use the in operator.

```
var song = {
  name: "Funky Shuffle",
  artist: "James Jackson",
  getArtist: function() {
    return song.artist;
  }
};
console.log("artist" in song); //true
console.log("getArtist" in song); //true
```

Cloning Objects

If you want to create an object that has access to another object's properties and methods, while being extensible, you can use the Object.create() function. The following example shows an object being cloned using this method.

```
var effects = {
  reverbs: {
    hall: "Hall reverb being used",
    plate: "Plate reverb being used",
    smallRoom: "Small room reverb being used"
  },
  guitar: {
    flange: "Flange being used",
    wahWah: "Wah wah being used"
  }
};

var updatedEffects = Object.create(effects);
console.log(updatedEffects.reverbs); //returns reverb object
console.log(updatedEffects.guitar); // returns guitar object
```

You can then extend the newly created object with properties and methods.

```
updatedEffects.filters = {
  lowPass: "Lowpass filter being used",
  highPass: "Highpass filter being used"
};
console.log(updatedEffects.filters); // returns filter object
console.log(effects.filters); // undefined
```

▮ Prototypal Inheritance

It is important to understand that Object.create() does not literally copy the
properties and methods to a new object but provides a reference to the properties
and methods contained in the parent object(s). This hierarchy of references between
objects is called *prototypal inheritance*. The following code shows this by cloning
multiple objects and including comments of the hierarchy of property accessibility.

```
var synth = {
  name: "Moog",
  polyphony: 32
};

var synthWithFilters = Object.create(synth); // clone synth
// synthWithFilters now has access to name and polyphony properties
synthWithFilters.filters = ["lowpass", "highpass", "bandpass"];
  // add property
/*The original synth object does not have access to the filters
  property.*/
var synthWithFiltersAndEffects = Object.create(synthWithFilters);
  // clone synthWithFilters
synthWithFiltersAndEffects.effects = ["reverb", "flange",
  "chorus"]; // add property
/*Neither the synth object nor the synthWithFilters object have
  access to the effects property*/
```

▮ The "this" Keyword

JavaScript contains a keyword called this that is used in methods to refer to an
object. In the following code, the method named nameAndArtist references
its containing object directly by using its name, which is song.

```
var song = {
  name: "Funky Shuffle",
  artist: "James Jackson",
  format: "wave",
  sampleRate: 44100,
  //_____BEGIN Method
  nameAndArtist: function() {
    return "Name: " + song.name + " | " + "Artist:" + song.artist;
  }
  //_____END Method
};
```

The reference to `song` can be replaced with the `this` keyword, and the result is the same.

```
nameAndArtist: function() {
  return "Name: " + this.name + " | " + "Artist: this.artist";
};
```

▐ The bind Function

The usefulness of the `this` keyword becomes apparent when you realize that *any function or method can be applied to any object.* The easiest way to demonstrate this is by using the built-in JavaScript method called `bind`. The `bind` method points a function's `this` value to the object specified in the first argument (the *bound* object). You can then invoke the function on the *bound* object. In the following code, `bind` points the `getName` function's `this` value to an object named `album`.

```
var song = {
  name: "Funky Shuffle",
  artist: "James Jackson",
  format: "wave",
  sampleRate: 44100
};

function getName() {
  return this.name;
}
var getNameOfSong = getName.bind(song); /*assign bound function to
  a variable*/
//_____Then invoke it!
console.log(getNameOfSong()); // Funky Shuffle
```

If you want to specify arguments in a function created with `bind`, you can do this in one of two ways. The first is to specify the arguments in the newly created function. In the following example, a function named `descriptor` is invoked on an object named `blastSound`. An argument is then passed to the `describeBlastSound` function.

```
var blastSound = {
   name: "Blast"
};

function descriptor(message) {
   return this.name + ": " + message;
}

var describeBlastSound = descriptor.bind(blastSound);
console.log(describeBlastSound("This is an explosive sound"));
   //Blast: This is an explosive sound
```

Alternatively, you can specify the arguments in the statement where you bind the function to the object. You do this by first specifying the object to bind to, then specifying arguments you want to use and separating them with commas, as in the following example:

```
var describeBlastSound = descriptor.bind(blastSound, "This is an
   explosive sound");
console.log(describeBlastSound()); /*Blast: This is an explosive
   sound*/
```

As you can see, even when a function has not been written as a method on a particular object, you can still apply the function to that object. This also means that you can use a method of one object and apply it to a completely different object. The following code uses a method named getNameAndArtist of an object named song and applies it to an object named Album.

```
var album = {
   name: "Funky Shuffle",
   artist: "James Jackson",
   format: "wave",
   sampleRate: 44100
};
var song = {
   name: "Analogue Heaven",
   artist: "The Keep It Reels",
   getNameAndArtist: function() {

      return "Name: " + this.name + " | Artist: " + this.artist;
   }
};
var getNameOfAlbum = song.getNameAndArtist.bind(album);
console.log(getNameOfAlbum()); /*Name: Funky Shuffle | Artist:
   James Jackson*/
```

If a function is invoked outside the context of an object, its this value points to one of two values, depending on whether strict mode is used or not. If strict mode is used, its this value is undefined. If strict mode is not used, its this value points to an invisible object called the *global* object, which contains all the built-in properties and methods of the web browser. You can view the value of `this` by using `console.log(this)` in the global scope without strict mode.

▌▌ Summary

In this chapter, you learned how to program with objects. In the next chapter, you will learn the basics of the Web Audio API node graph and working with oscillators.

7 Node Graphs and Oscillators

In previous chapters, you learned the basics of working with JavaScript data types and how to use the Web Audio API to generate basic tones. In this chapter, you will use your understanding of JavaScript to get a better understanding of two core features of the Web Audio API: node graphs and oscillators.

▌ The `AudioContext()` Method

The Web Audio API is accessed by using a collection of properties and methods of an object that you create using the `AudioContext()` method.

```
var audioContext = new AudioContext();
```

`AudioContext()` is a constructor that returns an object when you use the keyword new. Constructors and the new keyword are explained in Chapter 12. For now, the important thing to understand is that `AudioContext()` returns an object containing all of the methods and properties that you use to access the Web Audio API.

Node Graphs

A node graph is a collection of nodes. A node in a node graph is an object that represents an audio input source, such as an oscillator, or an object designed to manipulate an audio input source, such as a filter. These nodes are connected together using a method named `connect`.

The following code is an example of an oscillator node connected to a filter node.

```
"use strict";
var audioContext = new AudioContext();
//_____BEGIN create oscillator and filter
var filter = audioContext.createBiquadFilter();
var oscillator = audioContext.createOscillator();
//_____END create oscillator and filter
//_____BEGIN connect oscillator to filter
oscillator.connect(filter);
//_____END connect oscillator to filter
//_____BEGIN connect filter to computer speakers
filter.connect(audioContext.destination);
//_____END connect filter to computer speakers

//_____BEGIN start oscillator playing

oscillator.start(audioContext.currentTime);
//_____END start oscillator playing
```

In the previous code, the oscillator object is created using the `createOscillator` method of the audio context and stored in a variable named `oscillator`. You create the filter object in a similar way by invoking the `createBiquadFilter` method of `audioContext`. The `oscillator` is connected to the filter using `connect()`. The `filter` is connected to a property named `destination`. The `destination` represents the output of your computer's audio system. To start the oscillator playing, you use a method of the `oscillator` object named `start`. The `start` method takes one argument that determines the time the oscillator starts playing. The value of `audioContext.currentTime` is the current time in seconds within the Web Audio API, starting when `AudioContext` was invoked. (The topic of time is discussed in Chapter 20.)

Oscillators

Oscillators, like all Web Audio API nodes, have their own custom properties and methods. The following methods and properties are discussed in this chapter.

Method	Description
start	Starts oscillator playing
stop	Stops oscillator playing

Property	Description
onended	Executes a custom function when oscillator stops
type	Sets the type of waveform assigned to the oscillator
frequency	Sets the frequency value of the oscillator in hertz
detune	Sets an offset of the current frequency value in cents

The stop Method

The stop method determines when an oscillator stops. It takes one numeric argument that represents a time value in seconds. The following code starts an oscillator playing and stops it 3 seconds into the future.

```
var oscillator = audioContext.createOscillator();
oscillator.connect(audioContext.destination);
oscillator.start(audioContext.currentTime);
oscillator.stop(audioContext.currentTime + 3);
```

The onended Property

If you want to launch a function after the oscillator stop method has run, you assign that function to the onended property. The following code outputs the string "Oscillator has stopped" to the console after its stop method completes.

```
var oscillator = audioContext.createOscillator();
oscillator.connect(audioContext.destination);
oscillator.start(audioContext.currentTime);
oscillator.stop(audioContext.currentTime + 3);
oscillator.onended = function() {
  console.log("Oscillator has stopped");
};
```

How to Stop Oscillators and Restart Them

When an oscillator is stopped, it cannot be restarted. Instead, it must be recreated and then started. To demonstrate this, the following code attempts to restart an oscillator after it has stopped, which results in failure.

```
var audioContext = new AudioContext();
var oscillator = audioContext.createOscillator();
oscillator.connect(audioContext.destination);
oscillator.start(audioContext.currentTime);
oscillator.stop(audioContext.currentTime + 3);

oscillator.onended = function() {
  oscillator.start(audioContext.currentTime); // fails!
};
```

The following code recreates an oscillator and starts it playing 1 second after the previous oscillator stops.

```
var oscillator = audioContext.createOscillator();
oscillator.connect(audioContext.destination);
oscillator.start(audioContext.currentTime);
oscillator.stop(audioContext.currentTime + 3);

oscillator.onended = function() {
  oscillator = audioContext.createOscillator();
  oscillator.connect(audioContext.destination);
  oscillator.start(audioContext.currentTime + 1); /*start in
    one second*/
};
```

The `type` Property

The `type` property of an oscillator sets its waveform type in the form of a string. There are four predefined waveform shapes available.

- `sawtooth`

- `sine`

- `square`

- `triangle`

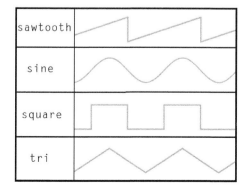

You assign a waveform type to an oscillator like this:

```
var audioContext = new AudioContext();
var oscillator = audioContext.createOscillator();
oscillator.connect(audioContext.destination);
oscillator.type = "sawtooth";
oscillator.start(audioContext.currentTime);
```

The default waveform type is sine.

The frequency Property

To set an oscillator's frequency, you must set the frequency property to a number. The frequency value is represented in hertz.

```
var oscillator = audioContext.createOscillator();
oscillator.connect(audioContext.destination);
oscillator.frequency.value = 80; //_____80 hertz
oscillator.start(audioContext.currentTime);
```

The detune Property

The detune property is expressed in cents. In the Western music scale, there are 100 cents per half-step note. This makes it easy to create musical note relationships using detune. The following code plays a note at a frequency of 130.81 hertz and is the frequency of a C3 note. The oscillator stops, and a half-second later a second note plays with the same frequency.value and a detune.value of 100 cents, making the note value C#3.

```
var audioContext = new AudioContext();
var oscillator = audioContext.createOscillator();
oscillator.connect(audioContext.destination);
oscillator.frequency.value = 130.81; //_____C3
oscillator.start(audioContext.currentTime);
oscillator.stop(audioContext.currentTime + 2);

oscillator.onended = function() {
  oscillator = audioContext.createOscillator();
  oscillator.frequency.value = 130.81; // C3 note
  oscillator.detune.value = 100; /*sets the note to one half step
    higher to C#3*/
  oscillator.connect(audioContext.destination);
  oscillator.start(audioContext.currentTime + 0.5);
  oscillator.stop(audioContext.currentTime + 2.5);
};
```

Summary

In this chapter, you learned the basics of node graphs and oscillators. In the next chapter, you will learn the basics of HTML and CSS and create the interface for your first Web Audio API applications.

8 Using HTML and CSS to Build User Interfaces

In this chapter, you will learn the basics of HTML and CSS, giving you the necessary tools to build user interfaces for your Web Audio API applications. You will do this by building a user interface intended to trigger an oscillator that includes interactive controls to select frequency and waveform type. In the next chapter, you will combine the interface with JavaScript code to build your first working interactive application.

What Is a User Interface?

A user interface, also called a *UI*, is the part of an application that a user interacts with. A music synthesizer's UI is the keyboard, as well as the knobs and sliders that allow you to modify the sound of the instrument. In a website or application, the UI can include buttons, form fields, sliders, scroll bars, and other elements that facilitate user control.

HTML

HTML stands for *hypertext markup language* and is the language used to create static websites. In Chapter 1, you learned that HTML consists of elements, sometimes referred to as *tags*, that make up the page of an HTML document. To be treated as an HTML document, a file must be saved with .html appended to its name. A file extension is a group of characters placed after a period in a file name that indicates the file's format. In the case of a file named `index.html`, the file extension is `.html`.

The following code is from the HTML template you created in Chapter 1. It consists of a collection of elements required to make a document W3C compliant. W3C stands for *World Wide Web Consortium*; this group is responsible for the development of web standards. Unlike JavaScript, HTML does *not* return errors if your code is written incorrectly, so you need additional tools to find HTML errors. You can test the compliance of an HTML document by running your code through the HTML validation tool at the following URL: https://validator.w3.org.

```html
<!DOCTYPE html>
<html>
  <head>
    <meta charset="UTF-8">
    <title>app</title>
    <script src="js/app.js"></script>
    <link rel="stylesheet" href="css/app.css">
  </head>
  <!--_____ BEGIN APP-->
  <body>

  </body>
  <!--_____ END APP-->
</html>
```

▮ Explanation of the HTML Template

The first element in an HTML file, `<!DOCTYPE>`, declares what version of HTML the page is written in. For HTML5, use `<!DOCTYPE html>`. As of this writing, HTML5 is the newest version of the HTML specification. The next element, `<html>`, encapsulates the remainder of the code. `<html>` represents the "root" of the document and contains the `<head>` and `<body>` elements. The `<head>` element describes information about the document, whereas the `<body>` element describes the content on the visible page.

Within the `<head>` element, the `<meta>` tag defines which keyboard character encoding is used on the web page. Character encodings represents the way that characters on your physical keyboard get translated to text. UTF-8 covers most languages and is also the standard for the modern web. The `<title>` element is used to give your page a title. The remaining code inside the `<head>` element includes references to external files that contain JavaScript and CSS code.

Immediately before the body element is a comment. HTML comments are written using the following syntax:

```html
<!--comment goes here -->
```

Inside the `<body>` element is where you write the bulk of your HTML code. In the following example, the `<p>` and `<h1>` elements between the opening and closing body tags show how HTML is used to display text. The `<h1>` element is a heading element and the `<p>` element is a paragraph element. As the names imply, you use the heading element to create title headings and the paragraph element to encapsulate text that represents a paragraph.

```
<!DOCTYPE html>
<html>
  <head>
    <meta charset="UTF-8">
    <title>Template</title>
    <script src="js/app.js"></script>
    <link rel="stylesheet" href="css/app.css">

  </head>
  <!--_____BEGIN APP-->
  <body>
    <h1> Creating an Interface </h1>
    <p>In this chapter we will go over HTML and CSS</p>
  </body>
  <!--_____END APP-->
</html>
```

▌▌ Understanding HTML Elements

In the HTML specification there are over 100 elements to choose from. Each one of these has a specific use case. A full list is available at the following URL: https://developer.mozilla.org/en-US/docs/Web/HTML/Element.

The sheer number of elements may be daunting at first, but once you understand how to use a small handful of these elements, it becomes easier to learn the others. For the purposes of this chapter, only the following elements are used:

`<div>`	**Div element**
	Defines a general-purpose block-level container
`<span>`	**Span element**
	Defines a general-purpose inline container
`<h1> to <h6>`	**Heading element**
	Creates a heading title
`<p>`	**Paragraph element**
	Wraps paragraph text
`<form>`	**Form element**
	Encapsulates input elements and denotes form fields
`<input>`	**Input element**
	Creates entry fields for forms
`<hr>`	**Horizontal rule element**
	Displays a horizontal line
`<ul>`	**Unordered list element**
	Contains list elements
`<li>`	**List item element**
	Contains text that is an item in a list

When you write HTML and CSS, you must understand two primary concepts. First, HTML web pages consist of a hierarchy of elements that form a nested tree-like structure. This is called the *HTML Document Object Model* (or *DOM* for short). The following diagram reflects the node tree of the previous example.

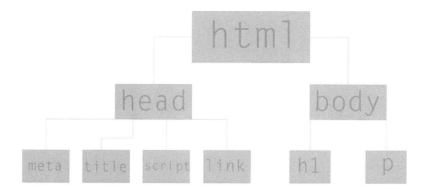

Second, most elements contain opening and closing tags that are used to encapsulate other elements. The processes of encapsulating elements within other elements and treating the containing elements as boxes is commonly referred to as the *box model*.

The following code emphasizes the box model by adding elements that contain other elements. This includes a containing <div> that encapsulates a <form> element. The <form> element then encapsulates <input>, <span>, and <p> (paragraph) elements.

```
<body>
  <h1> Creating an Interface </h1>
  <p>In this chapter we will go over HTML and CSS</p>
  <div>
    <form>
      <input id ="on-off" type = "button" value="start">
        <span>Click to start oscillator</span>
        <p>Use slider to modify frequency</p>
      <input type= "range">
    </form>
  </div>
</body>
```

The tree structure of the modified HTML is reflected in the following diagram.

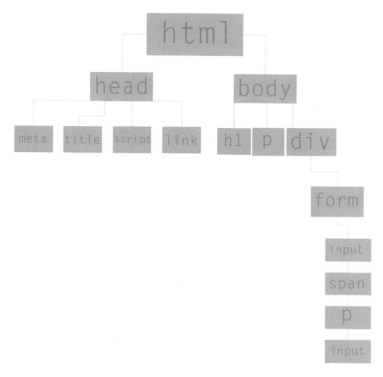

The rendering of the code looks like the following figure.

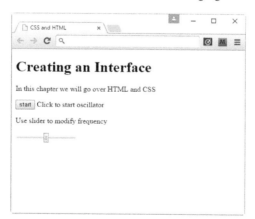

HTML elements come in two categories: *block-level* and *inline*. The difference between the two is that block-level elements display vertically and inline elements display horizontally. The <div> and <span> elements are two elements that reflect these characteristics. <div> is a block-level element and <span> is an inline element. These are both considered generic container elements. This means that they convey no special meaning but are useful to help lend structure to your page when no other elements are appropriate. The following code demonstrates how these elements are interpreted when they are rendered in the browser. The <hr> element is used solely to create a visual demarcation (horizontal line) between the two examples.

```
<body>
  <span>
  This text is inside a span
  </span>
  <span>
  This text is inside a span
  </span>
  <hr>
  <div>
  This text is inside a div
  </div>
  <div>
  This text is inside a div
  </div>
</body>
```

⊞ Form and Input Elements

<form> is a block-level element intended to encapsulate <input> elements. <input> elements are used to create text fields, buttons, and range sliders. The type attribute is used to define the type of data the element is expected to display, which can change how the element appears on the page. So for example, if you set the type attribute to range, it creates a slider.

```
<form>
  <input type = "range">
</form>
```

The `type` attribute comes with a built-in list of possible settings, some of which are shown in the following code. The `value` attribute gives the `<input>` element a default setting, as shown in the following demonstration code (code that is not used in your final application):

```
<body>
  <form>
    <p>Input element type set to "button"</p>
    <input type = "button" value="start">
    <hr>
    <p>Input element type set to "range"</p>
    <input type= "range">
    <hr>
    <p>Input element set to a "number"</p>
    <input type = "number" value="44.100">
    <hr>
    <p>Input element set to a "text"</p>
    <input type= "text" value ="sine">
  </form>
</body>
```

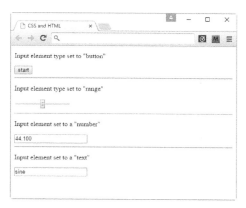

CSS

CSS stands for *cascading style sheets* and is the technology used to style web pages and web applications. Like HTML, CSS does not throw errors when written improperly. To check for errors, you can use the W3C CSS validator tool at this URL: https://jigsaw.w3.org/css-validator/.

CSS files use the `.css` file extension. To use CSS with an HTML file, you must first create a CSS document and then connect it to your HTML document using the `<link>` element in the `<head>`. The following example illustrates this usage, which is applied for the remainder of this chapter.

```
<!DOCTYPE html>
<html>
  <head>
    <meta charset="UTF-8">
    <title>CSS and HTML</title>
    <link rel="stylesheet" href="css/app.css">
  </head>
```

```
<body>
  <h1> Creating an Interface </h1>
  <p>In this chapter we will go over HTML and CSS</p>
  <div>
    <form>
      <input id ="on-off" type = "button" value="start">
      <span>Click to start oscillator</span>
      <p>Use slider to modify frequency</p>
      <input type= "range">
    </form>
  </div>
</body>
<html>
```

To ensure that your CSS document is being read properly, open your HTML document in Chrome and open the developer tools. If you made an error, the console will indicate this in red.

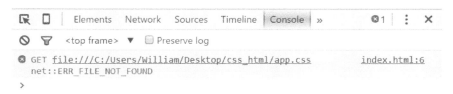

After the CSS file is linked you can begin to apply CSS styling to the HTML elements. For example, if you want to change the background color of the page, in your CSS file you select the body element and set the background-color property to a color value. This is shown in the following example where the background color is changed to orange. As an alternative to using the name of the color, you can set the color using a hex color code value such as #ffa500 or a red–green–blue value such as rgb(255,165,0).

```
body{
  background-color:orange;
}
```

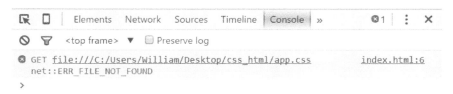

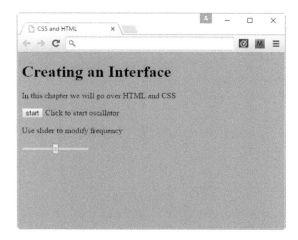

The procedure for applying CSS to an element is as follows:

1. Select the element you want to affect and type its name in your CSS file. In the previous example, this was body.

2. Type an opening and closing curly brace. These two braces are commonly referred to as a *code block*. Inside the code block you place properties and set values following a colon. In the previous example, the property was background-color and its value was orange. Each property value setting ends with a semicolon.

The CSS specification includes many properties. A full list of properties is available at this URL: https://developer.mozilla.org/en-US/docs/Web/CSS/Reference.

▌▌ Comments

Just like HTML or JavaScript, you can add comments to your CSS file using the following syntax:

```
/* This is a CSS comment */
```

▌▌ Element Selectors

When you select elements directly, *all* instances of the element are selected and the same CSS styling is applied to them. For example, in the following demonstration code, every <div> on the page is selected and given a background color of blue.

```
div{
  background-color:blue;
}
```

Grouping Selectors

If you want to apply the same styles to multiple selectors you can do so in one line of code by grouping selectors. You do this by separating each element with a comma. The following demonstration code selects the <p>, <li>, and <h1> elements and applies the same font color to each one.

```
p,li,h1{
    color:green; //Changes font color of all three elements to green
}
```

Descendent Selectors

If you want to access an element *only* if it is nested inside of a particular element, you can do this with descendent selectors. The CSS syntax for this type of selector is expressed by typing the parent element, a space, and then the element you want to select. In the following code, a descendant selector is used to select all <li> elements that are nested in any <div> element. In the following demonstration code, the font color of each <li> element is set to blue.

```
div li{
    color:blue;
}
```

It is important to realize that descendant selectors select all the descendent elements no matter how nested they are. If the previous CSS example were applied to the following HTML code, it would change the font color of all of the <li> elements to blue even though they are nested in a <ul> element.

```
<div>
    <ul>
        <li>Item-1</li>
        <li>Item-2</li>
        <li>Item-3</li>
    </ul>
</div>
```

Child Selectors

Child selectors are similar to descendent selectors with the difference that the selected element can only be *one* level deep relative to the parent. A child selector is made using the ">" symbol with the parent element on its left side and the child element on its right. The following demonstration code will select all <li> elements that are children of <ul> elements.

```
ul > li{
    /* do something */
}
```

class and id

Often when selecting elements, you do not want to select every element of a particular type. Rather, you might want to select either individual instances of elements or groups of elements. You can *single out* an individual element for styling by using an identifier called id. Conversely, you can designate a collection of elements as a *group* by using an identifier called class.

To single out an element using an id, you must first define id as an attribute of an HTML element. The syntax looks like the following:

```
<div id = "controls">
<!-- content -->
</div>
```

In your CSS you can then select this individual element by preceding its id with a hashtag character.

```
#controls{
  /* properties and values go here */
}
```

Keep in mind that id names are intended to be used only once in your HTML and are applied to a *single* element!

Modifying the App Interface

In the following code, an additional <div> is added to the page and encloses a collection of elements. You might be wondering why <h2> is used as the first element instead of another <h1>. The reason is that the number value of the heading element is intended to represent the precedence of the information contained within it. The lowest number is most important and each higher number is less important. So for example, the information contained in the <h1> element should take precedence because it conveys more overall meaning as it relates to the web page. You might notice that there is a size difference in the way the browser renders these elements. You should ignore this size difference and focus on content precedence. You can always change the font size using CSS to make these elements any size you want, including setting them all to the same size.

The next element is <ul> with an id of oscillator-list. This element contains a series of <li> elements, each given an id name of a particular waveform type. <ul> is an *unordered list* element and is intended to encapsulate the <li> elements, which are *list* elements. As the name implies, these elements are used to create lists.

```
<body>
  <h1> Creating an Interface </h1>
  <p>In this chapter we will go over HTML and CSS</p>
    <div>
      <form>
        <input id ="on-off" type = "button" value="start">
        <span>Click to start oscillator</span>
        <p>Use slider to modify frequency</p>
        <input type= "range">
```

```
    </form>
  </div>

  <div>
    <h2>Waveform</h2>
    <ul id="oscillator-list">
      <li id="sawtooth">sawtooth</li>
      <li id="sine"> sine</li>
      <li id="triangle">triangle</li>
      <li id="square">square</li>
    </ul>
  </div>
</body>
```

In the following CSS, each <li> element is selected via its id and given a background color.

```
#sawtooth{
  background-color: #336E91;
}
#sine{
  background-color: #783d47;
}
#triangle{
  background-color: #3b3040;
}
#square{
  background-color: #b85635;
}
```

Now that you know how to single out an element using id selectors, it is time to learn how to group elements using class selectors.

In your HTML document, assign the two <div> elements the class osc-controls. Then encapsulate the first <h1> and <p> inside a new <div>, and place another <div> element at the bottom of the page that contains a paragraph element with the phrase "JavaScript for Sound Artists Demo" inside of it.

You should have a total of four <div> elements in this code, which looks like this:

```
<body>
  <div>
    <h1> Creating an Interface </h1>
    <p>In this chapter we will go over HTML and CSS</p>
  </div>
  <div class="osc-controls">
    <form>
      <input id ="on-off" type = "button" value="start">
      <span>Click to start oscillator</span>
      <p>Use slider to modify frequency</p>
      <input type= "range">
    </form>
  </div>
  <div class="osc-controls">
    <h2>Waveform</h2>
    <ul id="oscillator-list">
      <li id="sawtooth">sawtooth</li>
      <li id="sine"> sine</li>
      <li id="triangle">triangle</li>
      <li id="square">square</li>
    </ul>
  </div>
  <div>
    <p>JavaScript for Sound Artists Demo</p>
  </div>
</body>
```

To select the osc-controls class from CSS, you must preface the class name with a dot.

```
.osc-controls{ /* Notice the dot selector */
  /* set property values */
}
```

In the following code, the osc-controls class is given a border. Only the middle two <div> elements respond to these changes because the first and third <div> on the page do not have the class osc-controls assigned to them.

```
.osc-controls {
  border-style:solid;
  border-color: #BC6527;
  border-width: 2px;
  border-radius:10px;
}
```

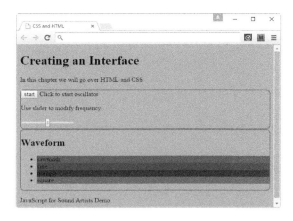

You might notice that the page looks a little awkward because the start button is now pushed up against the left edge of its container. Also, the two <divs> with borders are stacked directly on top of one another with no space between them. You could make this look a bit cleaner by creating some space between these elements. To do this, you should have an understanding of the following three properties: margin, border, and padding.

Margin, Border, and Padding

Both block-level and inline elements have access to `border`, `margin`, and `padding` properties, although they respond to them differently. These three properties correspond to three layers of space around an element. The `border` property creates a border around an element. The `padding` property creates a layer of space that resides inside the border. The `margin` property creates a layer of space that resides outside the border.

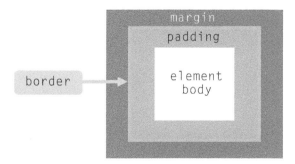

To create a bit of space between the text and a <div> element border, include the following code in your CSS file:

```
div{
  padding:20px;
}
```

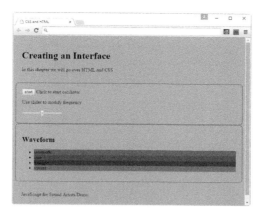

If you want to apply padding or a margin to only specific sides of an element, you can do so by using the following properties:

```
margin-top
margin-right
margin-bottom
margin-left
padding-top
padding-right
padding-bottom
padding-left
```

The two outlines around the middle <div> elements could use some space between them. The following code creates this space by using the bottom-margin property with a value of 20px.

```
.osc-controls {
  border-style:solid;
  border-color: #BC6527;
  border-width: 2px;
  border-radius:10px;
  margin-bottom:20px;
}
```

Removing List Element Bullet Points

The following code removes the bullet points from each list item by selecting all of the `<li>` elements that are descendents of an element with an `id` of `oscillator-list` and applying a property called `list-style-type` with a value of `none`.

```
#oscillator-list li{ /* Descendent selector */
    list-style-type: none;
}
```

You can remove the space previously occupied by the bullet points by setting the `padding-left` property to zero on the parent `<ul>` element.

```
#oscillator-list{
    padding-left:0px;
}
```

Font Size, Style (Type), and Color

As a touch-up, the following code selects all the elements that harbor text and sets their font size to `1.5em`, which is a bit larger than the current value. An em is equivalent to a parent element's font size, or, if there is no parent, the web browser's default text size. For most web browsers, this value is about 16 pixels, which in CSS is written as `16px`. Therefore, assuming there is no parent element, `2em` is equivalent to 32 pixels and `1.5em` to 24 pixels.

```
p,span,li,input{
    font-size:1.5em;
}
```

The default font type for Chrome is Times New Roman. You can change the font type if you like. The following code changes the font type to Arial.

```
body{
    background-color:orange;
    font-family: "Arial";
}
```

The font color of the text describing the waveform types is black, which is difficult to read because the background color of each <li> is dark. The following code changes the text color property to white.

```
#oscillator-list li{
  list-style-type: none;
  color:white;
}
```

■ Centering Block-Level Elements

If you want to center a block-level element, you can do so by setting its width to a value smaller than its containing element and applying a margin property with a value of 0   auto. This sets the left and right margin values to automatically extend to the boundaries of the container, centering the element. In the following code, a <div> with a class of application contains all the HTML within the body element. Its CSS is set to a fixed width and centered by specifying margin: 0 auto.

```
<body>
  <div class="application">
    <div>
      <h1> Creating an Interface </h1>
      <p>In this chapter we will go over HTML and CSS</p>
    </div>
    <div class="osc-controls">
      <form>
        <input id ="on-off" type = "button" value="start">
        <span>Click to start oscillator</span>
        <p>Use slider to modify frequency</p>
        <input type= "range">
      </form>
    </div>
    <div class="osc-controls">
      <h2>Waveform</h2>
```

```
    <ul id="oscillator-list">
      <li id="sawtooth">sawtooth</li>
      <li id="sine"> sine</li>
      <li id="triangle">triangle</li>
      <li id="square">square</li>
    </ul>
  </div>
  <div>
    <p>JavaScript for Sound Artists Demo</p>
  </div>
  </div>
</body>
```

The CSS for the newly created div is as follows.

```
.application{
  width:550px;
  margin:0 auto;
}
```

As a final step, remove the first <p> element and replace the text of the <h1> element with the title *Oscillator Generator*.

```
<div class="application">
  <div>
    <h1> Oscillator Generator </h1>
  </div>
  <div class="osc-controls">
    <form>
      <input id ="on-off" type = "button" value="start">
      <span>Click to start oscillator</span>
      <p>Use slider to modify frequency</p>
      <input type= "range">
    </form>
  </div>
  <div class="osc-controls">
    <h2>Waveform</h2>
    <ul id="oscillator-list">
```

```
    <li id="sawtooth">sawtooth</li>
    <li id="sine"> sine</li>
    <li id="triangle">triangle</li>
    <li id="square">square</li>
  </ul>
</div>
<div>
  <p>JavaScript for Sound Artists Demo</p>
</div>
</div>
```

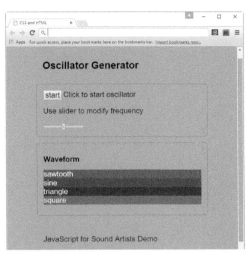

▐ Summary

In this chapter, you created the user interface for a small application. In the next chapter, you will add JavaScript code to make the application fully functional.

9 DOM Programming with JavaScript

This chapter shows you how to add JavaScript to CSS and HTML. By the end of the chapter, you will have created a fully functioning application with interactive controls.

How Does JavaScript Communicate with the DOM?

The DOM (Document Object Model) contains a collection of JavaScript properties and methods that allows you to manipulate HTML elements and to write code that responds to user-invoked actions such as mouse clicks and form submissions. Typically, when writing an application, you want to ask yourself two things. The first is, *what do you want or expect the user to do?* The second is, *what should happen in response to user actions?* So for example, the following code contains a play button, and when a user clicks it the browser runs a built-in function called `alert`. This function displays a pop-up with the message: You clicked play.

HTML

```
<body>
  <input id="play-button" type="button" value="PLAY">
</body>
```

JavaScript

```
window.onload = function() {
  var playButton = document.getElementById("play-button");
  playButton.addEventListener("click", function() {
    alert("You clicked the play button");
  });
};
```

The first line of JavaScript, `window.onload = function(){}`, restricts the code in the function scope from running until all of the HTML code has loaded. If the JavaScript were to load before the HTML, then any JavaScript intended to affect HTML elements or respond to user events like mouse clicks would either not be recognized or would be only partially recognized. The result in either of these cases is nonworking code.

The next line selects a DOM element with an `id` of `play-button` and stores it in a variable called `playButton`. This is done using `getElementById`, a method of the `document` object.

The `document` object is not part of the core JavaScript language. Instead, it is an object provided by the DOM API, making it part of the web browser.

```
var playButton = document.getElementById("play-button");
```

The next line of code applies the `eventListener` method to the `playButton`.

```
playButton.addEventListener("click", function() {
  alert("You clicked the play button");
});
```

The `playButton.addEventListener` method waits for a user to apply an action and then invokes a callback function. In this case, the action is a mouse click and is specified in the first argument of the function. The second argument is the callback. The callback runs when the user clicks on the element with the `id` of `play-button`, which invokes `alert()`.

The JavaScript DOM API contains many methods and properties. In this chapter, only the following of these are used.

Method or Property	Description
addEventListener	Allows elements to respond to user events such as mouse clicks
getElementById	Selects an element by id
getElementsByTagName	Selects elements by tag name
getElementsByClassName	Selects elements by class
classList.add	Adds a class to an element
classList.contains	Checks whether an element has a specified class name
classList.remove	Removes a class from an element
setAttribute	Sets an attribute on an element
innerHTML	Gets and sets the content of an element
value	Sets or gets the value of an input element

Building the Application

In the previous chapter, you built a user interface using CSS and HTML. You are now going to write the code to make this a working JavaScript application. To get started, create a copy of the final project in Chapter 8 and make sure you create a folder that contains a file named app.js. Your directory structure should look like the one in the following image.

In the app.js file, make sure you have strict mode enabled. All JavaScript code is written below the use strict string.

```
"use strict";
```

Set your index.html file to reference the app.js file.

```
<head>
  <meta charset="UTF-8">
  <title>CSS and HTML</title>
  <script src="js/app.js"></script>
  <link rel="stylesheet" href="css/app.css">
</head>
```

How to Trigger an Oscillator by Clicking a Button

The user interface you created in the previous chapter contained a button with the id of on-off. You are now going to write code to start an oscillator playing when this button is clicked.

```
"use strict";
var audioContext = new AudioContext();
window.onload = function() {
  var onOff = document.getElementById("on-off");
  onOff.addEventListener("click", function() {
    var osc = audioContext.createOscillator();
    osc.type = "sawtooth";
    osc.frequency.value = 300;
    osc.connect(audioContext.destination);
    osc.start(audioContext.currentTime);
  });
};
```

Although this code starts the oscillator playing, it does not *stop* it from playing. The following changes implement the stop feature by adding a conditional statement to `addEventListener` to check whether a variable named `osc` is set to false. If `osc` is false, an oscillator is created and assigned to it. This makes the Boolean value of the `osc` variable true, and the `start` method is invoked, allowing the oscillator to play. If the user clicks the **Start** button again, the conditional statement sees that the `osc` variable has the Boolean value `true` and runs the code in the `else` branch. This stops the oscillator from playing and resets `osc` to false.

```
"use strict";
var audioContext = new AudioContext();
window.onload = function() {
  var onOff = document.getElementById("on-off");
  /*_____BEGIN set initial
    osc state to false*/

  var osc = false;

  /*_____END set initial
    osc state to false*/
  onOff.addEventListener("click", function() {
    /*_____BEGIN Conditional
      statement to check if osc is TRUE or FALSE*/
    if (!osc) { /*_____Is osc false? If so then
      create and assign oscillator to osc and play it.*/

      osc = audioContext.createOscillator();
      osc.type = "sawtooth";
      osc.frequency.value = 300;
      osc.connect(audioContext.destination);
      osc.start(audioContext.currentTime);

      /*_____Otherwise stop it and
        reset osc to false for next time.*/
    } else {

      osc.stop(audioContext.currentTime);
      osc = false;
    }
    /*_____END Conditional
      statement to check if osc is TRUE or FALSE*/
  });
};
```

▌ Toggling the *Start/Stop* Text

Though the code in the previous example works, the following feature makes it more user-friendly: Program the button text and associated `span` element text to display the words *start* or *stop* depending on whether the oscillator is playing or not.

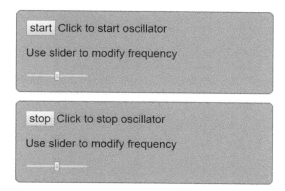

You can implement this feature as follows:

```
"use strict";
var audioContext = new AudioContext();
window.onload = function() {
  var onOff = document.getElementById("on-off");
  var span = document.getElementsByTagName("span")[0];

  /*_____BEGIN set initial osc
     state to false*/
  var osc = false;
  /*_____END set initial osc
     state to false*/

  onOff.addEventListener("click", function() {
    /*_____BEGIN Conditional
       statement to check if osc is TRUE or FALSE*/

    if (!osc) { /*_____Is osc false? If so then
         create and assign oscillator to osc variable and play it.*/
      osc = audioContext.createOscillator();
      osc.type = "sawtooth";
      osc.frequency.value = 300;
      osc.connect(audioContext.destination);
      osc.start(audioContext.currentTime);
      onOff.value = "stop";
      span.innerHTML = "Click to stop oscillator";
      /*_____Otherwise stop it and
         reset osc to false for next time.*/
    } else {

      osc.stop(audioContext.currentTime);
      osc = false;
      onOff.value = "start";
      span.innerHTML = "Click to start oscillator";
    }

    /*_____END Conditional
       statement to check if osc is TRUE or FALSE*/
  });
};
```

This code introduces a new DOM method called `getElementsBy-TagName` as well as two new DOM properties: `innerHTML` and `value`. The `getElementsByTagName` method allows you to select a collection of elements on the page by tag name. You can then specify an *individual* element using array-style index selectors. The index selection represents the order of the element on the page, with the first element starting at 0. To select the first span element on the page, you specify `getElementsByTagName("span")[0]`. If there are several span elements and you want to select the third one from the top of the page, you specify the index as 2, and the selector looks like this:

```
document.getElementsByTagName("span")[2]
```

It is important to understand that DOM elements are *not* arrays, even though the notation used to select them is similar to that used for arrays. DOM elements are referred to as *nodes*.

▮ Programming the Frequency Slider

You are now going to add functionality to the frequency slider. The following code shows how you capture the value of the frequency slider when the oscillator is clicked. This is done using the `value` property. The value is then stored in a variable named `freqSliderVal` and represents the frequency of the oscillator. Additionally, the `freqSliderVal` is logged to the console, allowing you to see changes made to it.

```
"use strict";
var audioContext = new AudioContext();
window.onload = function() {
  var onOff = document.getElementById("on-off");
  var span = document.getElementsByTagName("span")[0];

  /*_____BEGIN set initial osc
    state to false*/
  var osc = false;
  /*_____END set initial osc
    state to false*/
  onOff.addEventListener("click", function() {
    /*_____BEGIN Conditional
      statement to check if osc is TRUE or FALSE*/
    var freqSliderVal = document.getElementsByTagName("input")[1].
      value;

    console.log(freqSliderVal);

    if (!osc) { /*_____Is osc false? If so then
        create and assign oscillator to osc variable and play it.*/
      osc = audioContext.createOscillator();
      osc.type = "sawtooth";
      osc.frequency.value = freqSliderVal;
      osc.connect(audioContext.destination);
      osc.start(audioContext.currentTime);
      onOff.value = "stop";
```

```
    span.innerHTML = "Click to stop oscillator";
    /*_____Otherwise stop it and
        reset osc to false for next time.*/
} else {

    osc.stop(audioContext.currentTime);
    osc = false;
    onOff.value = "start";
    span.innerHTML = "Click to start oscillator";
}
/*_____END Conditional
    statement to check if osc is TRUE or FALSE*/
});
};
```

Changing the Frequency in Real Time

The code in the previous example works, but there is a cost. To hear the frequency changes, the user must turn the oscillator off, move the frequency slider, and then start the oscillator again. You could provide a seamless experience if the user could hear the effect in real time while moving the slider. To implement this, you can use setInterval() to check for state changes of the range slider and then apply them to the osc.frequency value.

The purpose of setInterval() is to invoke a function repeatedly at a specified time interval. In the following code, setInterval() takes two arguments. The first is a callback and the second is a number that represents a millisecond interval value (in this case, 50 ms). When setInterval() runs, the callback is invoked repeatedly at the time interval specified in the second argument. The freqSliderVal variable has been placed outside the scope of both the onOff.addEventListener and setInterval methods so that both of them have access to it. The setInterval method contains a conditional that checks to see whether osc is false, and if so displays the message "Oscillator is stopped. Waiting for oscillator to start," in the console. The moment the oscillator starts, setInterval() reassigns freqSliderVal to the respective <input> range value and assigns that value to osc.frequency. value. Because setInterval() does this in 50-ms increments, it creates near real-time change in the oscillator frequency when you move the frequency slider.

```
"use strict";
var audioContext = new AudioContext();
window.onload = function() {
  var onOff = document.getElementById("on-off");
  var span = document.getElementsByTagName("span")[0];
```

```
/*_____BEGIN set initial osc
  state to false*/
var osc = false;
/*_____END set initial osc
  state to false*/


/*_____BEGIN set initial
  frequency value*/
var freqSliderVal = document.getElementsByTagName("input")[1].
  value;
/*_____END set initial
  frequency value*/


/*_____BEGIN check range
  slider value and set frequency of oscillator*/

setInterval(function() {

  if (!osc) {

    console.log("Oscillator is stopped. Waiting for oscillator to
      start");

  } else {

    freqSliderVal = document.getElementsByTagName("input")[1].value;
    osc.frequency.value = freqSliderVal;
    console.log("Oscillator is playing. Frequency value is " +
      freqSliderVal);
  }

}, 50);

/*_____End check range slider
  value and set frequency of oscillator*/

onOff.addEventListener("click", function() {

  /*_____BEGIN Conditional
    statement to check if osc is TRUE or FALSE*/

  if (!osc) { /*_____Is osc false? If so then
    create and assign oscillator to osc variable and play it.*/
    osc = audioContext.createOscillator();
    osc.type = "sawtooth";
    osc.frequency.value = freqSliderVal;
    osc.connect(audioContext.destination);
    osc.start(audioContext.currentTime);
    onOff.value = "stop";
    span.innerHTML = "Click to stop oscillator";
    /*_____Otherwise stop it and
      reset osc to false for next time.*/
  } else {

    osc.stop(audioContext.currentTime);
    osc = false;
```

```
        onOff.value = "start";
        span.innerHTML = "Click to start oscillator";
    }

    /*_____END Conditional
      statement to check if osc is TRUE or FALSE*/
  });
};
```

Changing Waveform Types

You are now going to write code to allow users to click one of the four waveforms on the page and set the oscillator to play the selected waveform.

To do this, use the `eventListener()` method to capture the `id` of the element clicked by the user. Because the `id` of each `<li>` is the name of a waveform, you must assign this `id` to the `osc.type` property. You want users to be able to update the waveform type without having to repeatedly restart the oscillator, and you can do this similarly to the frequency slider changes in the previous example.

In the following code, you create a variable named `selectedWaveform` to give the oscillator a default waveform type and to store any selected waveform changes.

```
var selectedWaveform = "sawtooth";
```

This value is then assigned to `osc.type`.

```
if (!osc) {
  osc = audioContext.createOscillator();
  osc.type = selectedWaveform;
  osc.frequency.value = freqSliderVal;
  osc.connect(audioContext.destination);
  osc.start(audioContext.currentTime);
  onOff.value = "stop";
  span.innerHTML = "Click to stop oscillator";
}
```

Next, create a variable named `waveformTypes` and assign it the result of calling `getElementsByTagName()`. The `waveformTypes` value is used to select one of the four `<li>` elements on the page.

```
var waveformTypes = document.getElementsByTagName('li');
```

Next, create a function named `select` that is used as a callback for a series of event listeners used to select the `id` of the `<li>` clicked by the user.

```
function select() {
  selectedWaveform = document.getElementById(this.id).id;
  console.log(selectedWaveform); // Outputs id
}
```

Next, a `for` loop is used to examine each `<li>` node and assign an event listener to each one. Each event listener is set to respond to a click event that invokes the callback function `select`. When the `select` function runs, it captures the `id` of the `<li>` element clicked by the user. This `id` is then stored in the `selectedWaveform` variable.

```
for (var i = 0; i < waveformTypes.length; i++) {
  waveformTypes[i].addEventListener('click', select, false);
}
```

▌ Completed Code with Waveform Selection

```
"use strict";
var audioContext = new AudioContext();
window.onload = function() {
  var onOff = document.getElementById("on-off");
  var span = document.getElementsByTagName("span")[0];
  var osc = false;
  var freqSliderVal = document.getElementsByTagName("input")[1].value;

  /*_____BEGIN set selected
    waveform type value*/
  var selectedWaveform = "sawtooth";
  /*_____END set selected
    waveform type value*/

  /*_____BEGIN select all <li>
    elements*/
  var waveformTypes = document.getElementsByTagName('li');
  /*_____END select all <li>
    elements*/

  /*_____BEGIN callback to
    select <li> by id and assign id name to selectWaveform*/
  function select() {
    selectedWaveform = document.getElementById(this.id).id;
    console.log(selectedWaveform);
  }

  /*_____END callback to select
    <li> by id and assign id name to selectWaveform*/

  /*_____BEGIN loop through all
    <li> elements and set a click eventListener on them*/

  for (var i = 0; i < waveformTypes.length; i++) {
    waveformTypes[i].addEventListener('click', select);
  }
```

```
/*_____END loop through all
    <li> elements and set a click eventListener on them*/

setInterval(function() {

  if (!osc) {

    console.log("Oscillator is stopped. Waiting for oscillator to
      start");

  } else {

      freqSliderVal = document.getElementsByTagName("input")[1].
        value;
      osc.frequency.value = freqSliderVal;
      console.log("Oscillator is playing. Frequency value is " +
        freqSliderVal);
      osc.type = selectedWaveform;
  }

}, 50);

onOff.addEventListener("click", function() {

  if (!osc) {
    osc = audioContext.createOscillator();
    osc.type = selectedWaveform;
    osc.frequency.value = freqSliderVal;
    osc.connect(audioContext.destination);
    osc.start(audioContext.currentTime);
    onOff.value = "stop";
    span.innerHTML = "Click to stop oscillator";
  } else {

    osc.stop(audioContext.currentTime);
    osc = false;
    onOff.value = "start";
    span.innerHTML = "Click to start oscillator";
  }
});
};
```

▌ Giving an Outline to the Selected Waveform Type

When a user selects a waveform type, there is no visual cue that identifies
the type selected. The following code adds a white outline to the selected
waveform.

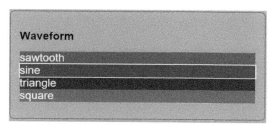

In the CSS file, create a class named `selected-waveform` and give it an outline property with a width of 2 pixels and the color white. Then, add this class dynamically to the `<li>` element that corresponds to the selected waveform type. To remove the selected waveform class of the previously selected element, use a for loop to examine all of the `<li>` elements and invoke `classList.remove("selected-waveform")` on each one.

In the CSS file, create the class.

```css
.selected-waveform{
  outline:2px solid white;
}
```

In the JavaScript file, add the following code to the `select` function.

```javascript
function select() {
    //_____BEGIN select element by id
    var selectedWaveformElement = document.getElementById(this.id);
    //_____END select element by id

    selectedWaveform = document.getElementById(this.id).id;
    console.log(selectedWaveform);

    /*_____BEGIN remove any
      previously added selected-waveform classes*/

    for (var i = 0; i < waveformTypes.length; i += 1) {
        waveformTypes[i].classList.remove("selected-waveform");
    }
    /*_____END remove any previously
      added selected-waveform classes*/

    /*_____BEGIN add the selected-
      waveform class to the selected element*/

    selectedWaveformElement.classList.add("selected-waveform");
    /*_____END add the selected-
      waveform class to the selected element*/
}
```

Summary

In this chapter, you learned how JavaScript interacts with the DOM. In the next chapter, you will learn the basics of a library named JQuery that makes DOM programming with JavaScript easier.

10 Simplifying DOM Programming with JQuery

In the previous chapter, you learned how JavaScript interacts with the DOM. In this chapter, you will learn how to simplify the process of adding interactive components to your application by using a library called *JQuery*. The objective of this chapter is not to teach you the entire JQuery API, but to give you the foundational knowledge to make JQuery a part of your programming toolkit. You can find the JQuery API at this URL: https://api.jquery.com/.

What Is JQuery?

JQuery is a library written in JavaScript intended primarily for DOM manipulation. A library is a collection of preassembled code pieces designed to make a particular group of tasks easier. JQuery contains a large collection of methods and properties that can be used individually or combined to help ease the complexity of JavaScript DOM programming.

JQuery Setup

You can set up JQuery in one of two ways. The first is to download the library and reference it from an HTML file. The second is to reference it from a content delivery network (*CDN* for short). A CDN is a service accessible through the World Wide Web where you can reference code libraries and other files. The downside of using a CDN is that you will always need a working Internet connection to access it.

Referencing JQuery Directly

To reference JQuery directly, first download the library at this URL: http://jquery.com/. Next, use the following code as an example of how to reference the library.

```
<!DOCTYPE html>
<html>
  <head>
    <meta charset="UTF-8">
    <title></title>
    <script type="text/javascript" src="js/jquery-2.1.4.min"
      charset="utf-8"></script>
    <script src="js/app.js"></script>
    <link rel="stylesheet" href="css/app.css">
  </head>
  <!--_____ BEGIN APP-->
  <body>

  </body>
  <!--_____ END APP-->
</html>
```

Using JQuery from a CDN

The following code references JQuery from a Google CDN library collection at this URL: https://developers.google.com/speed/libraries/.

```
<!DOCTYPE html>
<html>
  <head>
    <meta charset="UTF-8">
    <title></title>
    <script type="text/javascript" src="https://ajax.googleapis.
      com/ajax/libs/jquery/2.1.0/jquery.js" charset="utf-8">
    </script>
    <script src="js/app.js"></script>
    <link rel="stylesheet" href="css/app.css">
  </head>
  <!--_____ BEGIN APP-->
  <body>

  </body>
  <!--_____ END APP-->
</html>
```

In the previous chapter, your JavaScript code was encapsulated in the following function:

```
window.onload = function() {
  // code goes here
};
```

This was done to ensure that the code loads *after* the browser renders the HTML document. JQuery comes bundled with a function that does the same thing with slightly different syntax.

```
$(function(){
  // code goes here
});
```

How to Use JQuery

The most fundamental use cases for JQuery require knowledge of two things. The first is how to *select* an HTML element. The second is how to *do something* with that element.

Selecting HTML Elements

The following code shows how to select an HTML element.

```
$("div") // this selects all div elements on the page
```

The syntax for element selectors always begins with a dollar sign, followed by two parentheses. You place the element wrapped in quotes inside the parentheses. JQuery selectors borrow from CSS selector syntax. If you know how to select elements using CSS, you can quickly learn to select elements in JQuery. The following are a few examples of CSS selectors and their JQuery counterparts.

Selection Type	CSS	JQuery
Element	div{}	$("div")
Child	p > span{}	$("p > span")
Descendent	p span{}	$("p span")
Multi	div, span, p{}	$("div, span, p ")
id	#item{}	$("#item")
Class	.item{}	$(".item")

Storing DOM Selectors as Variables

In some circumstances, you might find it aesthetically preferable to store your DOM selectors as variables. The following code is a modified version of the previous example with the `div` selector stored in a variable. The variable is preceded by a dollar sign to emphasize that it is a JQuery selector. Storing the DOM selector as a variable has the same effect as selecting the element directly.

```
$(function() {
  var $transportControl = $("div");

});
```

▐ Using Methods

After you have selected an element, you can modify it in some way using JQuery's built-in methods. JQuery comes with a large collection of methods; however, in this chapter we are only going to use the following methods:

Method	Summary
on	Attaches event listeners to an element
css	Modifies the CSS of an element
fadeIn	Fades in an element over time
fadeOut	Fades out an element over time
val	Sets or gets the value attribute of an input element
addClass	Adds a class to an element
removeClass	Removes a class from an element
eq	Selects an element based on an index value
text	Sets or gets the text of an element

The following is an example of using `css()` to modify the look of an element. `css()` can be used either to change a single property or to set multiple properties using an object as an argument. An example of both use cases is given in the following code:

HTML

```
<div>Play</div>
<div>Stop</div>
<div>Rewind</div>
<div>Fast Forward</div>
<div>Pause</div>
```

To change a single property:

JQuery/JavaScript to Change a Single Property

```
$(function() {
  $("div").css("background-color","orange");
});
```

To change multiple properties:

JQuery/JavaScript to Change Multiple Properties

```
$(function() {
  $("div").css({
    backgroundColor:"orange",
    width:"100px",
    borderStyle:"solid"
  });
});
```

▌ Method Chaining

If you want to apply multiple methods to an element, you can connect them in succession so that they are invoked one after another. This is called *method chaining*.

In the following code, all of the div elements have their CSS display property set to none. JQuery is used to select the div elements and set their CSS properties using css(). The fadeIn method is then chained to each div, so that every div on the page fades in over the course of 1 second (1000 milliseconds). The first argument of fadeIn() is the duration of the animation in milliseconds. When fadeIn()completes, the fadeOut method is invoked, which fades out all div elements over the course of 1 second.

HTML

```
<div>Play</div>
<div>Stop</div>
<div>Rewind</div>
<div>Fast Forward</div>
<div>Pause</div>
```

CSS

```
div{
  display:none;
}
```

JQuery/JavaScript

```
$(function() {
  $("div").css({
    backgroundColor: "orange",
    width: "100px",
    borderStyle: "solid"
  }).fadeIn(1000).fadeOut(1000); // example of method chaining
});
```

The following HTML code contains an input element with its type attribute set to button. This is selected with JQuery and set to respond to click events *via* an event listener. The method used for this is on(), which takes two arguments.

The first argument is a string that defines the event type and the second is a callback that is invoked when the event is fired.

HTML

```
<input type="button" value = "Play">
```

JQuery/JavaScript

```
$(function() {
  $("input").on("click",function(){ //click event listener
    alert("You clicked play");
  });
});
```

The `this` Keyword

The `this` keyword in JQuery can be used as a shorthand for the currently selected DOM element. The following HTML code contains three input elements. Using JQuery, these three elements are assigned a click event listener. When a user clicks an input button, the $(this) selector is used to single out the individual element the user clicked. The `val` method returns the `value` attribute of the clicked element.

HTML

```
<input type="button" value = "Play">
<input type="button" value = "Pause">
<input type="button" value = "Stop">
```

JQuery/JavaScript

```
$(function() {
  $("input").on("click",function(){ /*assign event listener to all
    input elements*/
  console.log($(this).val()); /*use the this keyword to access the
    element clicked and return its value property*/
  });
});
```

Refactoring the Oscillator Player to Use JQuery

Now that you understand some JQuery basics, you are going to refactor the application you created in the previous chapter by replacing the built-in JavaScript DOM methods with JQuery selectors and methods.

Copy the completed code from the previous chapter to a new directory. In your index.html file reference the JQuery library.

```
<head>
  <meta charset="UTF-8">
  <title>CSS and HTML</title>
  <script type="text/javascript" src="https://ajax.googleapis.
    com/ajax/libs/jquery/2.1.0/jquery.js" charset="utf-8">
    </script>
  <script src="js/app.js"></script>
  <link rel="stylesheet" href="css/app.css">
</head>
```

Replace the `app.js` file with a new *empty* file with the same name.
In the old application, you used this function to encapsulate your code:

```
window.onload = function() {
}
```

In the new version of your code, make sure you replace `window.onload` with the equivalent JQuery function. Also put `"use strict"` and the `AudioContext` instantiation at the top of the file, as in the following example:

```
"use strict";
var audioContext = new AudioContext();
$(function() {
  // all code will go here
});
```

Next, modify the first three variables of the JavaScript file to use JQuery selectors.

Without JQuery

```
     app.js              ×
 1  "use strict";
 2  var audioContext = new AudioContext();
 3  window.onload = function() {
 4      var onOff = document.getElementById("on-off");
 5      var span = document.getElementsByTagName("span")[0];
 6      var osc = false;
 7      var freqSliderVal = document.getElementsByTagName("input")[1].value;
 8      var selectedWaveform = "sawtooth";
 9
10
```

With JQuery

```
     app.js              ×
 1  "use strict";
 2  var audioContext = new AudioContext();
 3
 4  $(function() {
 5      var $onOff = $("#on-off"); //_____JQuery selector
 6      var $messageText = $("span"); //_____JQuery selector
 7      var $freqSliderVal = $("input").eq(1).val(); //___JQuery selector
 8      var osc = false;
 9      var selectedWaveform = "sawtooth";
10
```

This code uses `$("#on-off")` to select the oscillator start or stop button by id. It is denoted by the hash selector. You then use `$("span")` to select the span that contains message text. This selection is done by element and, because there is only one span element on the page, you do not need to be more specific. Lastly, `$("input").eq(1).val()` is used to select the range slider value of the second input element on the page, which is stored in a variable named `$freqSlider-Val`. This is done by making a general element selection for all `input` elements and specifying the second one on the page with the `eq(1)` method. The `eq()` method enables selection of elements by index with its argument being the index value. Once the correct input element is selected, `val()` is used to get its *value* attribute.

▮▮ Setting Up the Event Listener for the User-Selected List Element

In the old application, the user interface code for oscillator selection was a bit complex. First, you needed to create a loop that attached a click event listener to all `<li>` elements. Then you created a function named `select` to be invoked as a callback for each of those event listeners. When the user clicked an `<li>` element, the `select()` callback looped through every `<li>` and removed any class identifiers titled `selected-waveform`. It then assigned the `selected-waveform` class to *only* the clicked element.

With JQuery, much of this complexity can be avoided. The following images show the contrast between the old version and a refined JQuery implementation.

Event Listener without JQuery

```
 1  "use strict";
 2  var audioContext = new AudioContext();
 3  window.onload = function() {
 4      var onOff = document.getElementById("on-off");
 5      var span = document.getElementsByTagName("span")[0];
 6      var osc = false;
 7      var freqSliderVal = document.getElementsByTagName("input")[1].value;
 8      var selectedWaveform = "sawtooth";
 9
10      //_____BEGIN select all <li> elements
11
12      var waveformTypes = document.getElementsByTagName('li');
13
14      function select() {
15          var selectedWaveformElement = document.getElementById(this.id);
16          selectedWaveform = document.getElementById(this.id).id;
17
18          for (var i = 0; i < waveformTypes.length; i += 1) {
19              waveformTypes[i].classList.remove("selected-waveform");
20          }
21
22          selectedWaveformElement.classList.add("selected-waveform");
23      }
24
25      for (var i = 0; i < waveformTypes.length; i++) {
26          waveformTypes[i].addEventListener('click', select);
27      }
28
29      //_____END select all <li> elements
30
```

Event Listener with JQuery

```
 1   "use strict";
 2   var audioContext = new AudioContext();
 3
 4   $(function() {
 5       var $onOff = $("#on-off"); //_____JQuery selector
 6       var $messageText = $("span"); //_____JQuery selector
 7       var $freqSliderVal = $("input").eq(1).val(); //____JQuery selector
 8       var osc = false;
 9       var selectedWaveform = "sawtooth";
10
11       //_____BEGIN <li> selection code
12
13
14       $("li").on("click", function() {
15           selectedWaveform = this.id;
16           $("li").removeClass("selected-waveform");
17           $(this).addClass("selected-waveform");
18
19       });
20
21       //_____END <li> selection code
22
```

The refactored JQuery code assigns a click event listener to all `<li>` elements. When the user clicks an `<li>` element, its id is stored in a variable named `selectedWaveform`. `selectedWaveform` is referenced in a higher scope and is used later to set the oscillator type. The `removeClass()` method is used to remove the selected-wavefrom class from *all* `<li>` elements. The last line of code uses `$(this)` to select the *specific* `<li>` the user clicked and invokes `addClass()` to give it the class selected-waveform.

▎ Modifying the Code in `setInterval`

The only modification you need to make to `setInterval` is the replacement of `freqSliderVal` with a JQuery DOM selector.

`setInterval` Method without JQuery

```
59
60       setInterval(function() {
61
62           if (!osc) {
63
64               console.log("Oscillator is stopped. Waiting for oscillator to start");
65
66           } else {
67
68               freqSliderVal = document.getElementsByTagName("input")[1].value;
69               osc.frequency.value = freqSliderVal;
70               console.log("Oscillator is playing. Frequency value is " + freqSliderVal);
71               osc.type = selectedWaveform;
72           }
73
74
75       }, 50);
76
```

setInterval Method with JQuery

```
23
24      setInterval(function() {
25          if (!osc) {
26              console.log("Oscillator is stopped. Waiting for oscillator to start");
27          } else {
28
29              $freqSliderVal = $("input").eq(1).val()
30              osc.frequency.value = $freqSliderVal;
31              console.log("Oscillator is playing. Frequency value is " + $freqSliderVal);
32              osc.type = selectedWaveform;
33          }
34      }, 50);
35
```

The remaining changes require you to modify the name of the onOff selector variable to $onOff and replace the addEventListener with the on() method set to respond to click events. Then rename the freqSliderVal to $freqSliderVal, replace the span.innerHTML with $messageText.text(), and lastly replace onOff.value with the JQuery equivalent of $onOff.val().

onOff Method without JQuery

```
80
81          onOff.addEventListener("click", function() {
82
83              if (!osc) {
84                  osc = audioContext.createOscillator();
85                  osc.type = selectedWaveform;
86                  osc.frequency.value = freqSliderVal;
87                  osc.connect(audioContext.destination);
88                  osc.start(audioContext.currentTime);
89                  onOff.value = "stop";
90                  span.innerHTML = "Click to stop oscillator";
91              } else {
92
93                  osc.stop(audioContext.currentTime);
94                  osc = false;
95                  onOff.value = "start";
96                  span.innerHTML = "Click to start oscillator";
97              }
98          });
99
100     };
```

$onOff Selector with JQuery

```
36
37          $onOff.on("click", function() {
38              if (!osc) {
39                  osc = audioContext.createOscillator();
40                  osc.type = selectedWaveform;
41                  osc.frequency.value = $freqSliderVal;
42                  osc.connect(audioContext.destination);
43                  osc.start(audioContext.currentTime);
44                  $onOff.val("stop");
45                  $messageText.text("Click to stop oscillator");
46              } else {
47
48                  osc.stop(audioContext.currentTime);
49                  osc = false;
50                  $onOff.val("start");
51                  $messageText.text("Click to start oscillator");
52              }
53
54          });
55
56      });
```

▮ Summary

In this chapter, you learned the basics of using JQuery for DOM manipulation. You also refactored the code in the previous chapter to contrast the difference between working with and without JQuery. In the next chapter, you will learn how to import and play back audio files with the Web Audio API.

11 Loading and Playing Audio Files

In this chapter, you will learn the basics of working with audio files. This includes how to load, play, and run audio files through the node graph to take advantage of its built-in effects.

■■ Prerequisites

To load and play back audio files, you must be running a web server. Chapter 1 gives you instructions about how to integrate a web server with Sublime Text by installing a package called Sublime Server. Your audio files are referenced from the directory the web server is pointing to, which you can set up as follows:

1. Create a folder on your desktop with a new project template.

2. Start the Sublime Text web server by selecting *Tools > SublimeServer > Start SublimeServer*.

3. Open the sidebar (if it isn't already open) by selecting *View > Side Bar > Show Side Bar*.

4. Drag the template folder to the side bar panel.

5. Open a web browser and enter: http://localhost:8080 in the URL field.

6. Click the link to the template folder. An empty screen is displayed because the initial template is empty.

For this exercise, you will need an audio file that is short and preferably of MP3 format (for compatibility issues). The file referenced in the example code is snare.mp3. Create a directory in your template folder and name it sounds, then copy your MP3 file there.

The Two Steps to Loading an Audio File

Loading an audio file is done in two steps:

1. Store the audio file in a buffer using the XMLHttpRequest object.

2. Decode the buffer with decodeAudioData.

In the first step, you use the built-in browser object named XMLHttpRequest to store the collected audio file in a *buffer*. This object is part of the web browser and is independent of the Web Audio API. A buffer is a small piece of internal memory used to store data so that it can be accessed quickly. Storing the file this way provides low latency playback and the ability to modify the raw waveform data, which is useful for some applications.

In the second step, you use the decodeAudioData method to *decode* the audio file buffer you created in the first step. After the Web Audio API has read and decoded the audio data, you can assign the object to a variable and reference it in the node graph for playback.

The following example shows how you load a single audio file, after which you can play it back by clicking on the browser window. The rest of this chapter is dedicated to explaining each line in this example and how all the lines work together.

```
var audioContext = new AudioContext();
var audioBuffer;
var getSound = new XMLHttpRequest();
getSound.open("get", "sounds/snare.mp3", true);
getSound.responseType = "arraybuffer";

getSound.onload = function() {
  audioContext.decodeAudioData(getSound.response, function(buffer) {
    audioBuffer = buffer;
  });
};

getSound.send();

function playback() {
  var playSound = audioContext.createBufferSource();
  playSound.buffer = audioBuffer;
```

```
    playSound.connect(audioContext.destination);
    playSound.start(audioContext.currentTime);
}
window.addEventListener("mousedown", playback);
```

▌█ The XMLHttpRequest Object

The first step to importing an audio file is to create a new XMLHttpRequest object. This object allows you to import data over the http protocol, which is the same protocol used to load web pages. This data can then be stored in various forms. The code to create the object is as follows:

```
var getSound = new XMLHttpRequest();
```

The XMLHttpRequest function invocation returns an object literal that is stored in a variable named getSound. This is done using the new keyword. The new keyword will not be covered until the next chapter, but don't worry. For now, the important thing is to understand that XMLHttpRequest is a function that returns an object. This object contains a large collection of built-in properties and methods. For loading sound files, you need five of these methods:

- open

- responseType

- onload

- response

- send

The next line of code uses the open method to fetch the audio file. This method has three arguments.

```
var getSound = new XMLHttpRequest();
getSound.open("get","sound/snare.mp3",true);
```

To clearly understand the purpose of the first argument requires a brief explanation of a command called a get request.

get Requests

When you type a URL into a web browser and "go" to a website, the web browser does not actually go anywhere. What actually happens is the browser issues a command to the website server that initiates a download of the HTML content and other files needed to view it. This command is called a get request. The beauty of get requests is that you can use them outside the context of typing a URL into a browser. In other words, you can write code to run get requests behind the scenes. This is how XMLHttpRequest is used to pull audio files into your application—and why the first argument of the open method is "get".

The second argument to the `open` method is the path to the file you want to fetch. For this example, an MP3 file named `snare.mp3` is imported.

A Word on Audio File Type Compatibility

It is important to understand that audio file type compatibility is dependent on which web browser you use. If you want your application to be compatible with multiple web browsers, you have to include multiple audio files of different formats *and* write conditional code to determine what format to use based on the rendering browser. The three most popular audio file formats for web browsers are WAV, OGG, and MP3. An audio file format compatibility chart for various browsers is available here: http://caniuse.com/#search=audio%20format.

The third argument to the `open` method determines whether the open operation is done in a synchronous or asynchronous manner. The `true` value selects the asynchronous setting, whereas `false` selects the synchronous setting. Understanding the difference between synchronous and asynchronous code execution is an in-depth topic and requires some explaining.

Synchronous *versus* Asynchronous Code Execution

When the browser executes code, it does so from top to bottom. As a result, a function that takes a long time to execute creates a noticeable delay in the program itself. This is because the code is executing synchronously.

When you use the `XMLHttpRequest` object to retrieve data *synchronously* from a server, the time delay between making the `get` request and when the actual data is returned can create a noticeable delay in the execution of your program. This delay is particularly noticeable when you load a large audio file and then have to wait for its entire contents to load into memory before your program continues.

Delays in execution are why doing such operations synchronously is discouraged and doing them *asynchronously* is preferred. Working asynchronously lets you run the open `method` while immediately allowing your program to continue executing to completion. In the meantime, the audio file continues to load behind the scenes, regardless of how long it takes to complete. When the audio file is available (when it is done loading), you can use it. When code is executed in this manner, we say that it is *nonblocking*. Of course, the downside of this is that if you have an audio file loading and it is taking a long time, the user of your program might be wondering why nothing is playing even though the page has rendered! This problem can be remedied by presenting a message to users to warn them that they will have to wait for the audio file to finish loading. In the meantime, they can explore other parts of your application.

The next line of code sets a property called `responseType` to a value of `arraybuffer`. The `responseType` property defines how the data you are importing is made available to your program. Generally, the `XMLHttpRequest` object is used to fetch text files, and in those cases you might choose one of the other available `responseType` settings such as `text` or `document`.

For sound files, `arraybuffer` is used. This is a general container for binary data that is useful for audio files.

```
var getSound = new XMLHttpRequest();
getSound.open("get","sounds/snare.mp3",true);
getSound.responseType = "arraybuffer";
```

The next line of code begins with an `onload` function that is invoked after the data (the audio file) has completed loading. Within the `onload` function, decoding of the audio data takes place that makes it usable by the Web Audio API. You do this with a method called `decodeAudioData` that takes two arguments. The first argument is a property called `response` that represents the loaded (and *undecoded*) audio data.

```
getSound.onload = function() {
  audioContext.decodeAudioData(getSound.response, function(buffer) {
    audioBuffer = buffer;
  });
};
```

The second argument to the `onload` function is a callback function that allows you to capture the result of the *decoded* audio data and do something with it. To capture the decoded file, you must pass it as an argument of the callback function. In this case, the name given for this decoded information is `buffer`. To make `buffer` accessible to the rest of the program, you can assign it to a global variable.

```
var audioContext = new AudioContext();
var audioBuffer;
var getSound = new XMLHttpRequest();
getSound.open("get", "snare.mp3", true);
getSound.responseType = "arraybuffer";
getSound.onload = function() {
  audioContext.decodeAudioData(getSound.response, function(buffer) {
    audioBuffer = buffer; // stored as global variable
  });
};
```

The last line is the send method. This method initiates the `XMLHttpRequest`.

```
getSound.send();
```

Now that the audio file is loaded into a buffer, the `playback` function contains the required code to connect it to the node graph and eventually play it back. The first line assigns a method called `createBufferSource` to a variable. This method is used to create a *buffer source node* that is used for audio buffers. In other words, it is like `createOscillator`, but instead of being used to create oscillators, it is used to create a node that can play back the contents of an audio buffer. To inject the audio buffer into the node graph, you need to assign it to a property of the buffer source node named `buffer`.

```
function playback() {

  var playSound = audioContext.createBufferSource();
  playSound.buffer = audioBuffer;
  playSound.connect(audioContext.destination);
  playSound.start(audioContext.currentTime);
}
```

You can now connect the buffer to the `audioConext.destination` and set the start time.

```
function playback() {

  var playSound = audioContext.createBufferSource();
  playSound.buffer = audioBuffer;
  playSound.connect(audioContext.destination);
  playSound.start(audioContext.currentTime);
}
```

The last line of code is an event listener that lets you play back the file when the window is clicked.

```
window.addEventListener("mousedown", playback);
```

If you click on the page, you should hear the audio file play.

Processing the Audio Buffer with the Node Graph

When the audio buffer is fed into the node graph, you can process it with its built-in effects. In the following code, the node graph connection has been modified to include a property of the audio buffer named `playbackRate`. This changes the playback speed of the sound. To double the speed, set the value to 2; to play the sound back at half speed, set the value to 0.5.

```
function playback() {
  var playSound = audioContext.createBufferSource();
  playSound.buffer = audioBuffer;
  playSound.playbackRate.value = 0.5;
  playSound.connect(audioContext.destination);
  playSound.start(audioContext.currentTime);
}
```

Summary

Each time you want to import an audio file into your program, you must initiate `XMLHttpRequest` with all the method and property settings shown in this chapter. You can imagine that duplicating this code repeatedly for each file is unfeasible for a large-scale application. By abstracting away this complexity, you can program a solution to this problem that lets you import multiple audio files with only a few lines of code. In the next two chapters, you will learn how to do this while learning about two new object creation methodologies: factories and constructors.

12 Factories and Constructors

In the previous chapter, you learned how to import audio files. You also learned that loading multiple files can require a tremendous amount of code duplication. Because repeating code is something that should be avoided, it is a good idea to abstract your audio file loading program into a library that imports all the required files with a minimal amount of code duplication. In this chapter, you will learn two new object creation patterns to help you do this. The first pattern, called *factory*, is used to create your audio loader library. The second pattern, called *constructor*, is introduced primarily because of its prevalence in the JavaScript world, making it an important pattern to familiarize yourself with. Factories and constructors are almost identical. The difference lies solely in minor implementation details and syntax. In other words, anything you can do with one of these patterns you can do with the other. Your choice of which to use comes down to personal choice.

In the next chapter, you will put what you learn here to work and build your audio file loading library.

▮▮ JavaScript and the Concept of *Class*

Programming languages that are organized around objects that interact with one another are usually referred to as *object oriented*. JavaScript is considered an object-oriented language, although it differs from traditional object-oriented languages in one important way: JavaScript lacks what are called *classes*.

What Are Classes?

With most object-oriented programming languages, to create an object you must first create a class, which is a kind of blueprint that your object is derived from. For example, imagine a class for a mixing console that contains a number of audio channels. When you create an object from this class, you have the option to determine the channel count on the fly. In this regard, the class acts as a kind of scaffolding for the creation of objects while offering a degree of flexibility for individual object customization.

The beauty of JavaScript is that when you create objects *directly*, you do not need classes. In fact, classes don't exist in JavaScript. However, if you want to program in a class-based style, you can do so easily with either of two available object creation patterns: factory and constructor.

The Factory Pattern

Factory is a fancy term for describing a function that returns an object.

```
function makeObj(){
    var obj = {};
    return obj;
}
var newObj = makeObj();
```

You can use factories to set properties and methods on the objects they return. In the following example, the factory `makeRecord` is used to create objects that represent music albums. With factories, property values are assigned to the returned object through function arguments. In the following example, the object's property values represent information about each record, including title, artist, and year.

```
function makeRecord(title, artist, year) {
    var record = {};
    record.title = title;
    record.artist = artist;
    record.year = year;

    return record;
}
var weAreHardcore = makeRecord("We Are Hardcore", "The Psycho
Electros", 2016);

console.log(weAreHardcore.title); // "We Are Hardcore"
console.log(weAreHardcore.artist); // "The Psycho Electros"
console.log(weAreHardcore.year); // 2016
```

If you want to create default values for properties, you can assign them like this:

```
function makeRecord(title, artist, year) {
    var record = {};
```

```
  record.title = title;
  record.artist = artist;
  record.year = year;
  record.fullAlbum = true;

  return record;
}

var weAreHardcore = makeRecord("We Are Hardcore",
  "The Psycho Electros", 2016);
console.log(weAreHardcore.fullAlbum); // true
```

You can also include methods in your factories.

```
function makeRecord(title, artist, year) {
  var record = {};
  record.title = title;
  record.artist = artist;
  record.year = year;
  record.summary = function() {
    return "Title:" + record.title + ". Artist:" + record.artist +
      ". Year:" + record.year;
  };

  return record;
}
var weAreHardcore = makeRecord("We Are Hardcore",
  "The Psycho Electros", 2016);

console.log(weAreHardcore.summary()); /*Title:We Are Hardcore.
  Artist:The Psycho Electros. Year:2016*/
```

▌█ Dynamic Object Extension

Objects created with factories, like all objects, can be extended to include additional properties and methods. The following example creates a new property named leadSinger and a new method named getAllProperties. getAllProperties loops through the object properties and logs those that are not functions to the console.

```
function makeRecord(title, artist, year) {
  var record = {};
  record.title = title;
  record.artist = artist;
  record.year = year;
  record.summary = function() {
    return "Title:" + record.title + ". Artist:" + record.artist +
      ". Year:" + record.year;
  };
  return record;
}

var weAreHardcore = makeRecord("We Are Hardcore",
  "The Psycho Electros", 2016);
```

```
weAreHardcore.leadSinger = "Fred The Butcher";
weAreHardcore.getAllProperties = function() {
  for (var prop in weAreHardcore) {
    if (typeof weAreHardcore[prop] != "function") {
      //_____Loop ignores methods!
      console.log(prop + ":" + weAreHardcore[prop]);
        //_____Only loops through properties
    }
  }
};

weAreHardcore.getAllProperties();

/*_____RESULT

title:We Are Hardcore
artist:The Psycho Electros
year:2016
leadSinger:Fred The Butcher

_____*/
```

Private Data

Sometimes you want to create data that is accessible to your objects but is either inaccessible to the outside scope or cannot be changed. To do this, you can make data private by assigning it to a variable inside the factory. In the following example, a variable named id stores some private information.

```
function makeRecord(id) {
  var id = id; // Private data
  console.log(id + " is private data");
  var record = {};
  return record;
}
var myRecord = makeRecord("2323415432");
console.log(myRecord.id); /*undefined. This is a property of the
  object, not the private data!*/
```

Getters and Setters

Private data can be retrieved by creating a method inside the factory that is designed to return it. A method used to retrieve private information is called a *getter*.

```
function makeRecord(id) {
  var id = id;
  var record = {};
  record.getId = function() { // getter
    return id;
  };
  return record;
}

var myRecord = makeRecord("1121210937");

myRecord.getId(); // 1121210937
```

12. Factories and Constructors

Conversely, methods that are used to modify private data are called *setters*. In the following code, a setter is created that allows you to change the value of `id` while restricting the input to a ten-digit string.

```
function makeRecord(id) {
  var id = id;
  var record = {};
  record.getId = function() {
    return id;
  };
  record.setId = function(newId) {
    if (typeof newId === "string" && newId.length === 10) {
      id = newId;
    } else {
      throw ("id must be a ten-digit string");
    }

  };
  return record;

}
var myRecord = makeRecord("9876543210");
myRecord.getId(); // 9876543210
myRecord.setId("1000000001");
myRecord.getId(); // 1000000001
```

Programming with factories is a common pattern in JavaScript and one that you should be sure to familiarize yourself with. Factories give you a simple syntax for abstracting complex code, while offering you the privacy of function scope coupled with the flexibility of object extension.

▮ Constructors and the new Keyword

Another pattern for object creation is called the *constructor*. Like a factory, a constructor is a function that returns an object. The following code shows an implementation of the makeRecord factory using a constructor.

```
function Record(title, artist, year) {
  this.title = title;
  this.artist = artist;
  this.year = year;
}
var weAreHardcore = new Record("We Are Hardcore",
  "The Psycho Electros", 2016);

console.log(weAreHardcore.title); // We Are Hardcore
console.log(weAreHardcore.artist); // The Psycho Electros
console.log(weAreHardcore.year); // 2016
```

As you can see, there are some differences between factories and constructors. The first is the naming convention for functions. With constructors, it is considered good practice to name them with a capitalized *noun*. This convention exists solely to help distinguish constructors from nonconstructors and does *not* throw an error if it is not used. The lack of an explicitly created object is the next difference. With constructors, instead of immediately creating an object in your function declaration, begin by writing your properties using the `this` keyword. In a constructor, `this` points to the object that is created from it. These properties are assigned values through the constructor function arguments or, if you want to create default values, you can assign them directly to the property.

```
function Record(title, artist, year) {
  this.title = title;
  this.artist = artist;
  this.year = year;
  this.fullAlbum = true; // default value
}

var weAreHardcore = new Record("We Are Hardcore",
  "The Psycho Electros", 2016);

console.log(weAreHardcore.fullAlbum); // true
```

You invoke a constructor using the `new` keyword. This is the command that tells the interpreter that you are using the function as a constructor. In response, the interpreter creates and returns an object. In the previous example, the return value is assigned to the variable named `weAreHardcore`.

▌ Adding Methods to Constructors

If you want to add methods to constructors, the syntax looks like this:

```
function Record(title, artist, year) {
  this.title = title;
  this.artist = artist;
  this.year = year;
}
Record.prototype.summary = function() {
  return "Title:" + this.title + ". Artist:" + this.artist +
    ". Year:" + this.year;
};

var weAreHardcore = new Record("We Are Hardcore",
  "The Psycho Electros", 2016);
weAreHardcore.summary(); /*Title:We Are Hardcore. Artist:The
  Psycho Electros. Year:2016*/
```

Admittedly, this syntax is a bit odd looking. So, to clarify what is happening, let's look at two concepts interwoven with constructors: the prototype *object* and the prototype *property*.

▌ The Prototype Object and the Prototype Property

Every time you create a function in JavaScript, a hidden object gets created in the background that is tied to the function that created it. This object is not visible or accessible and does absolutely nothing *unless* you decide to use your function as a constructor. If you use your function as a constructor, this otherwise dormant object becomes accessible through a property called *prototype* and is called the *prototype object*.

When you attach methods to constructors, you are expected to attach them to the prototype *property*, which in turns attaches them to the hidden prototype *object*. Any objects you create with your constructor have access to these methods.

```
Record.prototype.summary = function() {
  return "Title:" + this.title + ". Artist:" + this.artist +
    ". Year:" + this.year;
};
```

Although you can attach your methods without using the prototype property, the drawback to this approach is that every time you create a new object, all of the methods are initialized, and this requires more memory. This might have been a concern in 1995 when JavaScript was designed and computers were much slower, but the large amount of available memory in modern computers makes this issue negligible. This is the reason factories are a viable alternative. The syntax for adding methods without using the prototype object looks like this:

```
function Record(title, artist, year) {
  this.title = title;
  this.artist = artist;
  this.year = year;
  this.summary = function() {
    return "Title:" + this.title + ". Artist:" + this.artist +
      ". Year:" + this.year;
  };
}
```

```
var weAreHardcore = new Record("We Are Hardcore",
  "The Psycho Electros", 2016);
weAreHardcore.summary(); /*Title:We Are Hardcore. Artist:The
  Psycho Electros. Year:2016*/
```

You can use getters and setters, as you do with factories, to work with private data in constructors. The following example contains a private variable named id and uses a getter to retrieve it, as well as a setter that allows it to be changed to a ten-digit string. Note that the getter and setter are not implemented on the prototype property, because if they were, the private data would not be available to them.

```
function Record(id) {
  var id = id;
  this.getId = function() {
    return id;
  };

  this.setId = function(newId) {
    if (typeof newId === "string" & & newId.length === 10) {
      id = newId;
```

```
    } else {
      throw ("id must be a ten digit string");
    }

  };
}
var myRecord = new Record("9876543210");
myRecord.getId(); // 9876543210

myRecord.setId("0123456789");
myRecord.getId(); //0123456789
```

Why Do Constructors Exist If You Can Do the Same Thing with Factories?

At the time when JavaScript was developed in 1995, one of the most popular languages in the world was Java. Out of a desire to appease Java developers and lure them into using JavaScript, the language was designed to mirror Java's syntax. Part of this effort included adding constructors to the language that were designed to *look like* Java classes. This happened irrespective of the fact that behind the scenes JavaScript is not a class-based language.

Summary

In this chapter, you learned how to create JavaScript pseudoclasses using factories and constructors. In the next chapter, you will create a simplified audio file loader library using the factory pattern.

13 Abstracting the File Loader

Now that you are familiar with factories and constructors from the previous chapter, you can abstract the audio buffer loader you created in Chapter 11 into a library that loads multiple sound files using less code. You do this using the factory pattern.

▐▌ Thinking about Code Abstraction

Organizing your code into abstractions can be a daunting task. However, there are two steps you can follow to simplify the process. The first step is to determine whether you need an abstraction in the first place. If you are repeatedly typing out a large amount of code for the same task, then the answer is probably *yes*. The second step, if you decide you need an abstraction, is to determine what type of interface works for your abstraction. You were exposed to one example of a popular interface in Chapter 11, where you worked with the JQuery library. JQuery's interface allows you to treat HTML elements as objects that you can attach methods to. This is an excellent choice for an interface, but sometimes a simple function invocation that returns a string or number works just as well. Ultimately, it depends on your objective and the nature of the code you are abstracting.

One way to help you decide on the best approach is to work backward and *write out how you would like the interface to look and function prior to implementing it.* The interface for the audio file abstraction you create in this chapter looks like the following example:

```
var sound = audioBatchLoader({
  kick: "kick.mp3",
  snare: "snare.mp3",
  hihat: "hihat.mp3",
  shaker: "shaker.mp3"
});
sound.snare.play(); // Play
```

With this approach, a factory function takes an object as an argument. The object you input into the factory contains a list of property names, each of which is assigned a directory of an audio file in the form of a string. The beauty of this approach is its clarity and extensibility. The interface shown in `sound.snare.play()` attempts to read, somewhat like English, from the list of sound files to play. Even if you have never seen this code before, you can understand what it is doing: selecting a sound named `snare` and playing it. Decoupling the object that contains many audio files from the invoking function makes the code easier to read, as shown in the following example:

```
var audioFiles = {
  kick: "kick.mp3",
  snare: "snare.mp3",
  hihat: "hihat.mp3",
  shaker: "shaker.mp3"
  //_____hundreds of audio files could be listed here........
};

var sound = audioBatchLoader(audioFiles);
sound.snare.play(); // Play
```

If the user of your abstraction decides they want to extend it to do new things, without having to modify the source code in the original function, they have some flexibility. So for example, if they wanted to extend the returned object to play multiple audio buffers, they could do this:

```
sound.playSnareAndShaker = function() {
  sound.snare.play();
  sound.shaker.play();
};

sound.playSnareAndShaker(); // plays two sounds with one line of code
```

Creating the Abstraction

The following code is the *finished* abstraction. The remainder of this chapter is dedicated to building up this example line by line and explaining how it works. Create a new template project and save the following code in the JavaScript folder in a file named `audiolib.js`.

```
"use strict";

var audioContext = new AudioContext();
```

```javascript
function audioFileLoader(fileDirectory) {
  var soundObj = {};
  var playSound = undefined;
  var getSound = new XMLHttpRequest();
  soundObj.fileDirectory = fileDirectory;
  getSound.open("GET", soundObj.fileDirectory, true);
  getSound.responseType = "arraybuffer";
  getSound.onload = function() {
    audioContext.decodeAudioData(getSound.response, function(buffer) {
      soundObj.soundToPlay = buffer;

    });
  };

  getSound.send();

  soundObj.play = function(time) {
    playSound = audioContext.createBufferSource();
    playSound.buffer = soundObj.soundToPlay;
    playSound.connect(audioContext.destination);
    playSound.start(audioContext.currentTime + time ||
      audioContext.currentTime);
  };

  soundObj.stop = function(time) {
    playSound.stop(audioContext.currentTime + time || audioContext.
      currentTime);
  };
  return soundObj;
}

function audioBatchLoader(obj) {

  for (var prop in obj) {
    obj[prop] = audioFileLoader(obj[prop]);

  }

  return obj;

}

var sound = audioBatchLoader({

  kick: "sounds/kick.mp3",
  snare: "sounds/snare.mp3",
  hihat: "sounds/hihat.mp3",
  shaker: "sounds/shaker.mp3"

});

window.addEventListener("mousedown", function() {
  sound.snare.play();
});
```

You now need to reference the file in your index.html file.

```html
<head>
  <meta charset="UTF-8">
  <title></title>
```

```
      <script src="js/audiolib.js"></script>
      <script src="js/app.js"></script>
      <link rel="stylesheet" href="css/app.css">
</head>
```

Create a folder named sounds. This is the directory used to hold your audio files.

▌▌ Walking through the Code

The function named audioFileLoader creates and returns an object named soundObj.

```
function audioFileLoader(){
  var soundObj = {};
  return soundObj;
};
```

To specify a directory for the file to be used, a parameter is assigned to a property of soundObj named fileDirectory.

```
function audioFileLoader(fileDirectory){
  var soundObj = {};
  soundObj.fileDirectory = fileDirectory;
  return soundObj;
};
```

You can now create the XMLHttpRequest object and set all the required properties and methods. You can also implement the decodeAudioData method to make the buffer usable by the Web Audio API. These lines of code should already be familiar to you because they are the same buffer loading and decoding tools you learned about in Chapter 11, with one small difference. In Chapter 11 the decoded buffer was assigned to a variable named audioBuffer. In this implementation, the decoded buffer is assigned to a property of soundObj named soundToPlay.

```
function audioFileLoader(fileDirectory) {
  var soundObj = {};
  var getSound = new XMLHttpRequest();
  soundObj.fileDirectory = fileDirectory;
  getSound.open("GET", soundObj.fileDirectory, true);
```

```
    getSound.responseType = "arraybuffer";
    getSound.onload = function() {
      audioContext.decodeAudioData(getSound.response, function(buffer) {
        soundObj.soundToPlay = buffer; // Property assigned buffer

      });
    };

    getSound.send();
    return soundObj;
}
```

You can now create a playback method that is an extension of soundObj to play back the buffers.

```
function audioFileLoader(fileDirectory) {

    var soundObj = {};
    soundObj.fileDirectory = fileDirectory;
    var getSound = new XMLHttpRequest();
    getSound.open("GET", soundObj.fileDirectory, true);
    getSound.responseType = "arraybuffer";
    getSound.onload = function() {
      audioContext.decodeAudioData(getSound.response, function(buffer) {
        soundObj.soundToPlay = buffer;

      });
    };

    getSound.send();

    soundObj.play = function(time) {

      var playSound = audioContext.createBufferSource();
      playSound.buffer = soundObj.soundToPlay;
      playSound.connect(audioContext.destination);
      playSound.start(audioContext.currentTime + time ||
        audioContext.currentTime);
    };

    return soundObj;

}
```

The time argument of the play function determines the number of seconds you want the audio file to play into the future. The logical expression (audio-Context.currentTime + time || audioContext.currentTime) is used to determine whether the time argument is empty and, if it is, then the start method does not add additional seconds to the value of audioContext.currentTime. When no arguments are set, the sound plays immediately.

```
soundObj.play = function(time) {

    var playSound = audioContext.createBufferSource();
    playSound.buffer = soundObj.soundToPlay;
    playSound.connect(audioContext.destination);
```

```
    playSound.start(audioContext.currentTime + time ||
        audioContext.currentTime);
};
```

The stop method lets users determine when a sound will stop playback.

```
soundObj.stop = function(time) {
  playSound.stop(audioContext.currentTime + time ||
      audioContext.currentTime);
}
```

You can now load the files and play them.

```
var sound = audioFileLoader("sounds/snare.mp3");
window.addEventListener("mousedown", function() {
  sound.play(); // plays at "current time" because no arguments are set
  sound.play(2); // plays 2 seconds into the future
});
```

This code works, but it reveals a new potential problem. If you want to load multiple files, you have to type out an audioFileLoader invocation for each one, like this:

```
var kick = audioFileLoader("sounds/kick.mp3");
var snare = audioFileLoader("sounds/snare.mp3");
var hihat = audioFileLoader("sounds/hihat.mp3");
var shaker = audioFileLoader("sounds/shaker.mp3");
```

One way to mitigate this additional repetition is to create a helper function that loops through an object that contains a collection of audio file directories and invoke the audioFileloader on each file. You can then return the object. This will allow each sound to be accessible *via* its property name. The following code demonstrates this:

```
function audioBatchLoader(obj) {
  for (var prop in obj) {
    obj[prop] = audioFileLoader(obj[prop]);
  }
  return obj;
}

var sound = audioBatchLoader({
  kick: "sounds/kick.mp3",
  snare: "sounds/snare.mp3",
  hihat: "sounds/hihat.mp3",
  shaker: "sounds/shaker.mp3"
});
```

Each file is now accessible using the following syntax:

```
sound.kick.play();
sound.snare.play();
sound.hihat.play();
sound.shaker.play();
```

You now have a working library to load multiple audio files. The following code sets an event listener on the window. If you click it, you will hear the loaded sound play.

```
var sound = audioBatchLoader({

  kick: "sounds/kick.mp3",
  snare: "sounds/snare.mp3",
  hihat: "sounds/hihat.mp3",
  shaker: "sounds/shaker.mp3"

});

window.addEventListener("mousedown", function() {

  sound.snare.play();

});
```

▌ Summary

In this chapter, you learned the basics of how to think about abstraction, while creating a new tool for loading and playing back multiple audio files. In the next few chapters, you will learn how to manipulate audio *via* the node graph using various effects.

14 The Node Graph and Working with Effects

Up to this point, the topic of the *node graph* has only been partially described and has been used mostly as a tool to explain related concepts. In this chapter, you will learn how to work with the node graph to develop custom signal chains for complex audio applications. The Web Audio API includes many built-in objects that let you manipulate audio in creative ways. You also learn how to include these objects in your applications and use them to create customized effects.

▮ How to *Think About* the Node Graph

In a real-world recording studio, you route audio signals by connecting microphones and other sound sources to a sound mixer. The sound mixer is configured with its own routing scheme, which allows access to equalizers, dynamics processors, and other effects. The Web Audio API node graph is designed to mirror the characteristics of a real-world sound mixer. This is done by connecting input sources such as oscillators and audio buffers to other objects that manipulate the sonic characteristics of these input sources in some way. The various objects (including the input sources) that make up the signal chains are called *nodes* and are connected to one another using a method named connect(). You can think of connect() as a virtual audio cable used to chain the output of one node to the input of another node. The final end point connection for any Web Audio application is always going to be the audioContext.destination. You can think of the audioContext.destination as the *speakers* of your application. This collection of connections is what is referred to as the *node graph*, shown in the figure below.

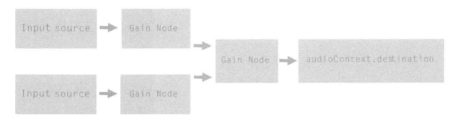

▌ Gain Nodes

In a real-world recording studio, you typically use a sound mixer with multiple channel strips and a routing matrix to split and combine audio signals. With the Web Audio API node graph, you use *gain nodes* to split and combine *input sources*. Gain nodes allow independent volume control over input sources and act as virtual mixing channels.

The following code is an example of creating two oscillators and connecting each one to an independent gain node for individual volume control. These are summed to a third gain node, which is connected to the audioContext. destination.

```
//_____BEGIN create sawtooth oscillator
var oscSaw = audioContext.createOscillator();
oscSaw.type = "sawtooth";
oscSaw.frequency.value = 118;
oscSaw.start(audioContext.currentTime);
//_____END create sawtooth oscillator

/*_____BEGIN create gain node and
  connect sawtooth oscillator*/

var gainSaw = audioContext.createGain();
gainSaw.gain.value = 0.6; // set volume
oscSaw.connect(gainSaw);

/*_____END create gain node and connect
  sawtooth oscillator*/
```

```
/*_____BEGIN create triangle wave
   oscillator*/
var oscTri = audioContext.createOscillator();
oscTri.type = "triangle";
oscTri.frequency.value = 120;
oscTri.start(audioContext.currentTime);
/*_____END create triangle wave
   oscillator*/

/*_____BEGIN create gain node and
   connect triangle wave oscillator*/

var gainTri = audioContext.createGain();
gainTri.gain.value = 3; // set volume
oscTri.connect(gainTri);

/*_____END create gain node and connect
   triangle wave oscillator*/

//____SUM Both Oscillators___
var gainOscSum = audioContext.createGain();
gainOscSum.gain.value = 1;
gainTri.connect(gainOscSum);
gainSaw.connect(gainOscSum);
//____Connect to the audioContext.destination
gainOscSum.connect(audioContext.destination);
```

The Placement of Nodes Is Up to You

It is important to realize that due to the flexible nature of the node graph, you can place your input sources and other nodes at any part of the chain. Imagine you have ten gain nodes all connected in series, and you want to inject an oscillator into the sixth one. This is perfectly fine because the oscillator is unaffected by the first five gain nodes in the chain by being funneled through the last five gain nodes prior to reaching the audioContext.destination. This is not just a feature of gain nodes but the nature of the node graph. *You can place any input source, or any other node, anywhere you want in the node graph signal chain.* The order in which you connect objects is dependent on the result you want.

What Effects Are Available?

The following chart contains some of the nodes that are characteristic of the effect processors you see in real-world recording studios. These effects are called *modification nodes,* but for clarity they are referred to as *effects nodes* in this book. The specifics of effects nodes are explored in later chapters. The focus of this chapter is to give you a general understanding of how these effects nodes can be incorporated into the node graph.

Node Name	Effect	Description
Gain	Volume modification	Sets the volume of an input source. Gain nodes are also used as virtual mixing channels that can be connected in parallel or in series.
StereoPanner	2D equal power panning	Changes the stereo placement of sound in 2D space.
BiquadFilter	EQ filter	Accentuates or attenuates part of the frequency spectrum of an input source.
Delay	Audible delay	Creates a time delay between when an input source plays and when the signal is made audible.
Convolver	Convolution reverberation	Creates reverberation effects by referencing impulse response files that model real-world spaces. Can also be used creatively for nonreverb applications.
DynamicsCompressor	Dynamic range compression	Modifies the volume of a signal dynamically.

How to Determine the Nodes You Need to Create the Effect You Want

If you have an idea for an effect you want to incorporate into your application, you can follow these steps to help determine the tools you need to create it:

1. Determine the specific type of effect you want (chorus, tremolo, hall reverberation, multiband, EQ, etc.).

2. Determine the nature of the effect. In other words, if the effect you want is a chorus, then the nature of the effect is an audible delay. If the effect you want is a multiband equalizer, then the nature of the effect is audio filtering.

3. Research the Web Audio API specification to find a node that you can use to create the effect. Many times, creating the exact effect you want requires combining different nodes or combining similar nodes with slightly modified parameters.

4. Invoke the respective method of the AudioContext to create the node (or nodes if you are using more than one). This is a method that starts with the word *create*, such as createGain() or createBiquadFilter().

5. Connect the object (or objects if you are using more than one) to the node graph in the part of the signal chain that you want.

6. Modify the built-in properties and methods of the object(s) to manipulate the input source(s) in the manner you want.

A Real-World Example

Assume you want to apply a low-pass (also called *lowpass*) filter to an oscillator. (A low-pass filter is a filter that only allows signals below a certain frequency to pass.) To do this, you first research the Web Audio API documentation to see whether this type of filter is supported. You can search the specification directly at: https://www.w3.org/TR/webaudio. An alternative reference (and one that is a bit more readable) is the Mozilla Developer Network documentation at: https://developer.mozilla.org/en-US/docs/Web/API/Web_Audio_API.

When researching, do a search for "filters" or "lowpass." In the results, you will discover that there is a specialized node called a *biquad filter* that is dedicated to audio filtering. This node includes a property named type that you can set to lowpass. As the value implies, this filter type is used to apply a low-pass filter to an input source. To apply this to your application, you first invoke the createBiquadFilter() method, which returns an object that you store in a variable. You then connect an input source, such as an oscillator or array buffer, to this object using the connect method.

```
var audioContext = new AudioContext();

var osc = audioContext.createOscillator();
osc.start(audioContext.currentTime);
var filter = audioContext.createBiquadFilter();
filter.type = "lowpass";
osc.connect(filter);
filter.connect(audioContext.destination);
```

The final step is to define any additional properties or methods to customize the effect. Properties or methods that allow you to customize the behavior of nodes are called *audio params* (short for *audio parameters*). In the previous example, type is an audio param. The following code sets another audio param named frequency to the value 250. This defines where the low-pass filter begins to cut off in the frequency spectrum.

```
var audioContext = new AudioContext();

var osc = audioContext.createOscillator();
osc.start(audioContext.currentTime);
var filter = audioContext.createBiquadFilter();
filter.type = "lowpass"; // audio param
filter.frequency.value = 250; // audio param
osc.connect(filter);
filter.connect(audioContext.destination);
```

Some Effects Require Development Work

It is important to understand that the Web Audio API's effects nodes are *building blocks*. This means that some of the effects you want to achieve might require additional development work on your part. For example, if you want to use a multiband equalizer, you won't find a "multiband equalizer node" in the Web Audio API specification. Instead, you must build your own multiband equalizer using a collection of `BiquadFilter` nodes.

▌▌ Summary

In this chapter, you were formally introduced to the node graph and how to create custom signal chains using input sources and effects nodes. In the next few chapters, you will build on this knowledge and explore the specifics of some of these effects nodes.

15 The Biquad Filter Node

One of the most common ways to manipulate sound is by boosting or attenuating a range of frequencies using audio filters. A familiar example of this is the use of audio equalizers to brighten or muffle a sound. The Web Audio API has a node named BiquadFilter that allows you to create different types of audio filters that can be connected together to create various forms of equalizers. In this chapter, you will learn how to use the BiquadFilter node, and in the process, you will create a seven-band graphic equalizer and a single-band parametric equalizer.

▪▪ Using the Biquad Filter Node

To use the BiquadFilter node, you must first instantiate it using the create BiquadFilter function and store the returned object in a variable.

```
var audioContext = new AudioContext();
var filter = audioContext.createBiquadFilter();
```

Once you create the object, you can connect an input source to it. The following example connects an oscillator to the object.

```
var audioContext = new AudioContext();
var osc = audioContext.createOscillator();
var filter = audioContext.createBiquadFilter();
```

```
osc.connect(filter); // connect input source to filter
osc.start(audioContext.currentTime);
filter.connect(audioContext.destination); /*connect filter to
  audioContext.destination*/
```

▮ Filter Types

BiquadFilter contains a property named type that defines the type of filter the node behaves like. If you do not explicitly set the type property, its default value is lowpass. You can see this in the console.log() output in the following code:

```
var audioContext = new AudioContext();
var osc = audioContext.createOscillator();
var filter = audioContext.createBiquadFilter();
filter.frequency.value = 250;
console.log(filter.type); // default is lowpass
osc.connect(filter);
osc.start(audioContext.currentTime);
filter.connect(audioContext.destination);
```

To explicitly set the type property to lowpass, you write the following code:

```
filter.type = "lowpass";
```

In addition to the type property, BiquadFilter has a property named frequency.value that allows you to assign a particular frequency to the object. The value is in hertz and is represented by a number. The default value is 350.

```
filter.frequency.value = 1000; // 1000 Hz or 1kHz
```

The type value of a BiquadFilter node determines if it has two additional properties: gain and Q. The gain.value property allows you to boost or attenuate frequency.value. The Q.value property represents the bandwidth of the frequency value. Bandwidth represents the reach by which neighboring frequencies are affected in relation to changes made to the gain of the selected frequency. The following images demonstrate the difference between a narrow bandwidth setting and a wide bandwidth setting of a 1 kHz frequency using a peaking filter.

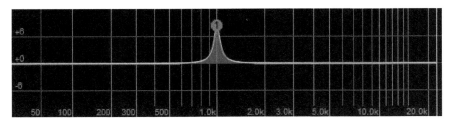

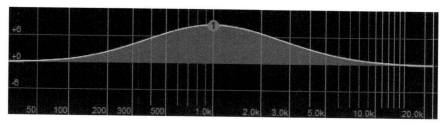

The effect `Q.value` and `gain.value` have on `frequency.value` depends on the filter's `type` setting. The following chart lists the available filter types and describes the relationship between `type`, `frequency`, `Q`, and `gain` properties.

Type	Description	Frequency	Q	Gain
lowpass	Frequencies below the cutoff are allowed to pass through. Frequencies above the cutoff are attenuated.	The cutoff frequency.	The larger the value, the greater the peak produced.	*Not used*
highpass	Frequencies above the cutoff are allowed to pass through. Frequencies below the cutoff are attenuated.	The cutoff frequency.	Sets the width of the frequency band. The greater the number, the narrower the value.	*Not used*
bandpass	Frequencies inside the range of frequencies pass through. Frequencies outside the range are attenuated.	The center of the range of frequencies.	Sets the width of the frequency band. The greater the number, the narrower the value.	*Not used*
lowshelf	Frequencies lower than the upper limit get a boost or an attenuation depending on the gain setting.	The upper limit of the frequencies receiving the boost or attenuation.	*Not used*	Creates a boost in decibel. If the value is negative, the gain is attenuated.
highshelf	Frequencies higher than the lower limit get a boost or an attenuation depending on the gain setting.	The lower limit of the frequencies getting a boost or an attenuation.	*Not used*	Creates a boost in decibel. If the value is negative, the gain is attenuated.
peaking	Frequencies inside a range of frequencies are boosted or attenuated depending on the gain setting.	The middle of the frequency range getting a boost or an attenuation.	Sets the width of the frequency band. The greater the number, the narrower the value.	Creates a boost in decibel. If the value is negative, the gain is attenuated.

Continued

Type	Description	Frequency	Q	Gain
notch	Frequencies inside a range of frequencies are not allowed to pass through.	The center of the range of frequencies.	Controls the width of the frequency band. The greater the Q value, the smaller the frequency band produced.	*Not used*
allpass	Allows all frequencies through but changes their phase relationship.	The frequency where the center of the phase transition occurs.	Controls how sharp the transition is at the selected frequency. The larger this value, the sharper the transition produced.	*Not used*

Creating an Equalizer

Two of the most common types of equalizers are parametric and graphic. A graphic equalizer allows you to boost or attenuate a series of *fixed* frequencies but does not include the ability to modify the bandwidth of those selected frequencies. Parametric equalizers, on the contrary, allow you to select a specific frequency, boost or attenuate it, and change the bandwidth range. You can use BiquadFilter nodes to design either of these equalizers, and many others.

Graphic EQ

The following diagram and code show how to create a seven-band graphic equalizer. You do this by chaining a series of BiquadFilter nodes together and setting their type properties to peaking. Keep in mind that the only parameter the user of a graphic equalizer should be allowed to change is the gain of each filter. The input and output source for this example is abstracted using a function named multibandEQ.

```
var filter1 = audioContext.createBiquadFilter();
filter1.type = "peaking"; /*_____Do not let user modify. This is a
   graphic EQ!*/
filter1.gain.value = 0;
filter1.Q.value = 1; /*_____Do not let user modify. This is a
   graphic EQ!*/
filter1.frequency.value = 64; /*__Do not let user modify. This is a
   graphic EQ!*/

var filter2 = audioContext.createBiquadFilter();
```

```
filter2.type = "peaking"; /*_____Do not let user modify. This is a
    graphic EQ!*/
filter2.gain.value = 0;
filter2.Q.value = 1; /*_____Do not let user modify. This is a
    graphic EQ!*/
filter2.frequency.value = 150; /*_Do not let user modify. This is a
    graphic EQ!*/

var filter3 = audioContext.createBiquadFilter();
filter3.type = "peaking"; /*_____Do not let user modify. This is a
    graphic EQ!*/
filter3.gain.value = 0;
filter3.Q.value = 1; /*_____Do not let user modify. This is a
    graphic EQ!*/
filter3.frequency.value = 350; /*_Do not let user modify. This is a
    graphic EQ!*/

var filter4 = audioContext.createBiquadFilter();
filter4.type = "peaking"; /*_____Do not let user modify. This is a
    graphic EQ!*/
filter4.gain.value = 0;
filter4.Q.value = 1; /*_____Do not let user modify. This is a
    graphic EQ!*/
filter4.frequency.value = 1000; /*Do not let user modify. This is a
    graphic EQ!*/

var filter5 = audioContext.createBiquadFilter();
filter5.type = "peaking"; /*_____Do not let user modify. This is a
    graphic EQ!*/
filter5.gain.value = 0;
filter5.Q.value = 1; /*_____Do not let user modify. This is a
    graphic EQ!*/
filter5.frequency.value = 2000; /*Do not let user modify. This is a
    graphic EQ!*/

var filter6 = audioContext.createBiquadFilter();
filter6.type = "peaking"; /*_____Do not let user modify. This is a
    graphic EQ!*/
filter6.gain.value = 0;
filter6.Q.value = 1; /*_____Do not let user modify. This is a
    graphic EQ!*/
filter6.frequency.value = 6000; /*Do not let user modify. This is a
    graphic EQ!*/

var filter7 = audioContext.createBiquadFilter();
filter7.type = "peaking"; /*_____Do not let user modify. This is a
    graphic EQ!*/
filter7.gain.value = 0;
filter7.Q.value = 1; /*_____Do not let user modify. This is a
    graphic EQ!*/
filter7.frequency.value = 12000; /*Do not let user modify. This is a
    graphic EQ!*/

function multibandEQ(inputConnection, outputConnection) {

  inputConnection.connect(filter1);
  filter1.connect(filter2);
  filter2.connect(filter3);
```

```
filter3.connect(filter4);
filter4.connect(filter5);
filter5.connect(filter6);
filter6.connect(filter7);
filter7.connect(outputConnection);

}
```
The code files for this chapter include versions of both the graphic and para-metric equalizers with user interface controls. These applications allow you to toggle the playback of a song and change parameters of the BiquadFilter nodes in real time by using the interactive sliders.

▮▮ Parametric EQ

You can design a parametric equalizer in a similar way to the graphic equal-izer by chaining a series of BiquadFilter nodes together and setting their type properties to peaking. The primary difference of the parametric equalizer is that the frequency, gain, and bandwidth are modifiable by the user. Keep in mind that with multiband parametric equalizers, the filter type may have mul-tiple options available. To keep the code simple and short, the following example shows how to create a *single*-band parametric equalizer with type set to the value peaking. The input and output source in this code is abstracted using a func-tion named parametricEQ.

```
var parametricEQ1 = audioContext.createBiquadFilter();
parametricEQ1.type = "peaking";
parametricEQ1.gain.value = 0; // allow the user to change this
parametricEQ1.Q.value = 1; // allow the user to change this
parametricEQ1.frequency.value = 1000;
function parametricEQ(inputConnection, outputConnection) {
  inputConnection.connect(parametricEQ1);
  parametricEQ1.connect(outputConnection);
}
```

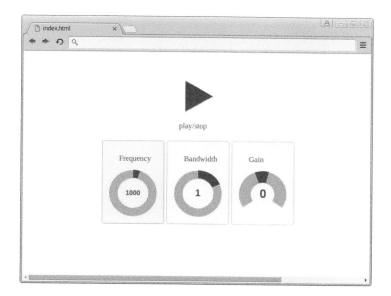

▌ Summary

In this chapter, you learned about the `BiquadFilter` node and how to use it to create custom equalizers and filter arrangements. Keep in mind that the examples here are kept simple, and like the node graph itself, your filter arrangements can be as complex as you want to make them. In the next chapter, you will learn about another signal processing node: the convolver node.

16 The Convolver Node

In this chapter, you will learn how to use the convolver node. The convolver allows you to apply reverberation to node graph input sources by referencing a special kind of audio file called an impulse response.

▌▌ Convolution Reverb

When an acoustic sound is created, its characteristics are shaped by its immediate environment. This is due to sound waves bouncing off and around various obstacles. These obstacles can be made of different materials that affect the sound in different ways. The result of sound emanating from a small room has different characteristics than sound emanating from a large room. Because the human ear can hear these differences, when this information is transmitted to the brain, we perceive these characteristics as room *ambience*. Modern advancements in digital audio technology allow us to record the ambience of any real-world environment and apply it to any digital audio signal directly. These *recorded ambiences* are stored as a special file called an impulse response. An impulse response file is made by recording a single sound burst in an environment, which could be white noise, a sine wave sweep, or even a balloon pop. This recording is then run through a special digital algorithm to create a single file called an impulse response. This impulse response file is combined *or convolved* with another input source to give the targeted sound the spacial characteristics of the room that the impulse is modeled from.

The format of impulse response files can be any audio file type including WAV, MP3, AIFF, or OGG. However, to use them with the Web Audio API, impulse response files must be in a browser-compatible audio format. For this chapter, we use WAV files because they are of higher quality than MP3 files. And because impulse response files are small, load time is not a concern.

Where to Get Pre-Recorded Impulse Response Files

There are many online resources where you can download impulse response files for free, such as: http://www.openairlib.net/.

Using Impulse Response Files

To use impulse response files, you must first load them, decode them, and store them in a buffer.

```
var audioContext = new AudioContext();
var impulseResponseBuffer;
var getSound = new XMLHttpRequest();
getSound.open("get", "sounds/impulse.js", true); // impulse file
getSound.responseType = "arraybuffer";

getSound.onload = function() {
  audioContext.decodeAudioData(getSound.response, function(buffer) {
    impulseResponseBuffer = buffer;
  });
};
getSound.send();
```

After the file is stored in a buffer, the next step is to wire up the necessary nodes to apply the effect to an input source. To integrate the impulse response into the node graph configuration, you must first create a convolver node using `audioContext.createConvolver()` and store the returned object in a variable.

```
var convolver = audioContext.createConvolver();
```

You then assign the loaded impulse response buffer to the buffer property of the object.

```
convolver.buffer = impulseResponseBuffer;
```

Next, you connect any input source you want to the convolver node. Here is an example of connecting an oscillator.

```
var osc = audioContext.createOscillator();
var convolver = audioContext.createConvolver();
osc.type = "sawtooth";
convolver.buffer = impulseResponseBuffer;
osc.connect(convolver);
convolver.connect(audioContext.destination);
osc.start(audioContext.currentTime);
```

The following HTML and JavaScript code combines the impulse file loader, node graph connections, and JQuery DOM selectors to allow you to play the oscillator by clicking an HTML button and holding it. This allows you to hear the reverberation effect more explicitly because the reverb tail is audible after removing your finger from the mouse button and stopping the oscillator.

HTML

```
<!DOCTYPE html>
<html>
  <head>
    <meta charset="UTF-8">
    <title></title>
    <script type="text/javascript" src="https://ajax.googleapis.
      com/ajax/libs/jquery/2.1.0/jquery.js"></script>
    <script src="js/app.js"></script>
  </head>
  <body>
    <button>Oscillation</button>
  </body>
</html>
```

JavaScript

```
"use strict";
var audioContext = new AudioContext();
var impulseResponseBuffer;
var getSound = new XMLHttpRequest();
getSound.open("get", "sounds/impulse.wav", true);
getSound.responseType = "arraybuffer";

getSound.onload = function() {
  audioContext.decodeAudioData(getSound.response, function(buffer) {
    impulseResponseBuffer = buffer;
  });
};

getSound.send();

/*_____BEGIN playback
  functionality*/

var osc = audioContext.createOscillator();
```

```
function playback() {
  var convolver = audioContext.createConvolver();
  osc = audioContext.createOscillator();
  osc.type = "sawtooth";
  convolver.buffer = impulseResponseBuffer;
  osc.connect(convolver);
  convolver.connect(audioContext.destination);
  osc.start(audioContext.currentTime);
}

$(function() {

  $("button").on("mousedown", function() {
    playback();
  });

  $("button").on("mouseup", function() {
    osc.stop();
  });
});
```

Controlling the Amount of Reverberation

In the previous code example, the amount of reverb applied to the oscillator is fixed at 100 percent. If you want to make the effect variable, which allows you to control how much of the effect is applied to the input source, you can do so by splitting the input source with a gain node and routing one split to the convolver node prior to connecting it to the destination. You then connect the other split directly to the destination. You use gain.value to blend the amount of the effect you want to hear.

The following diagram and node graph configuration code demonstrate the splitting operation.

```
var gain = audioContext.createGain();
var convolver = audioContext.createConvolver();

osc = audioContext.createOscillator();
osc.type = "sawtooth";
convolver.buffer = impulseResponseBuffer;
osc.connect(convolver);
convolver.connect(gain);
gain.gain.value = 0.2;
gain.connect(audioContext.destination);
osc.connect(audioContext.destination);
osc.start(audioContext.currentTime);
```

▮ Summary

In this chapter, you learned how to use the convolver node to apply an impulse response file to an input source. You also learned how to use gain nodes to control the amount of the effect you want to hear. In the next chapter, you will learn how to modify the panning of stereo input sources and how to create sophisticated routing schemes using the channel and merger nodes.

17 Stereo Panning, Channel Splitting, and Merging

The Web Audio API includes a stereo panner node that lets you pan input sources to any part of the stereo field. It also includes nodes that let you split multichannel audio files into separate channels as well as merge multichannel input sources into a specified output channel. In this chapter, you will learn how to use these nodes to manipulate multichannel input sources.

▍▐ The Stereo Panner Node

To use the stereo panner node, you first invoke `createStereoPanner()` and store the returned object in a variable.

```
var stereoPanner = audioContext.createStereoPanner();
```

You can then connect any input source to the node and use `pan.value` to set the location in the stereo field where you want to place the sound. The `pan.value` property setting is a number between 1 and –1, where 1 represents a 100 percent pan to the right and –1 represents a 100 percent pan to the left. In the following example, an oscillator is connected to a stereo panner node and is set 50 percent to the left.

```
var oscillator = audioContext.createOscillator();
var stereoPanner = audioContext.createStereoPanner();
```

```
stereoPanner.pan.value = -0.5;
oscillator.connect(stereoPanner);
stereoPanner.connect(audioContext.destination);
oscillator.start(audioContext.currentTime);
```

The `stereoPanner()` uses an equal power algorithm to pan input sources. This means that when a stereo input source is panned, the audio content on the attenuated side is *summed* with the audio on the amplified side.

▍ The Channel Splitter

If you want to isolate the individual channels of a multichannel input source or do not want your stereo input sources to be subjected to an equal power algorithm, you must use the channel splitter. This node isolates any channel of a multichannel input source for further processing. This applies to both stereo and other multichannel audio input sources, such as 5.1 surround files. To create a channel splitter, you invoke the `createChannelSplitter()` method with a single argument and store the returned object in a variable. The argument value is the number of channels of the audio source material that you intend to connect to the splitter. If no argument is specified, the default is 6. In the following example, a stereo file is split, so the argument is set to 2.

```
var splitter = audioContext.createChannelSplitter(2);
```

To use the channel splitter, you connect input sources to it and then connect the splitter to other nodes. When connecting the splitter to a destination node, you specify the channel of the input source to connect to in the second argument of the `connect()` method. This argument is a number that represents the channel as an index value. The following chart displays the index for each channel of a six-channel input source.

Channel	Index Value
L	0
R	1
SL	2
SR	3
C	4
LFE	5

The following code shows the correspondence between the channel index argument and its respective channel type.

```
stereoInputSource.connect(splitter);
splitter.connect(audioContext.destination, 0); /*outputs left
    side/channel of stereo input source*/
splitter.connect(audioContext.destination, 1); /*outputs right
    side/channel of stereo input source*/
```

The following code shows how to modify the gain value of individual left and right channels of a stereo input source. In other words, this configuration is the opposite of an equal power panning algorithm.

```
var splitter = audioContext.createChannelSplitter(2);
var pannerLeft = audioContext.createStereoPanner();
var pannerRight = audioContext.createStereoPanner();
var left = audioContext.createGain();
var right = audioContext.createGain();
sound = audioContext.createBufferSource();
sound.loop = true;
sound.buffer = bufferSource;
sound.connect(splitter);
splitter.connect(left, 0); //___connect left channel to gain node
splitter.connect(right, 1); //__connect right channel to gain node
left.gain.value = leftVal; /*_____independent left channel
    control*/
right.gain.value = rightVal; /*_____independent right channel
    control*/
left.connect(pannerLeft);
pannerLeft.pan.value = -1;
pannerRight.pan.value = 1;
right.connect(pannerRight);
pannerLeft.connect(audioContext.destination);
pannerRight.connect(audioContext.destination);
sound.start(audioContext.currentTime + time || audioContext.
    currentTime);
```

▮ The Channel Merger

If you want to combine multiple mono input sources and route them to a specific channel in the stereo (or multichannel) spectrum, you use a channel merger. The function invocation for the channel merger node takes one argument that determines how many input channels the object accepts. If no argument is given, the default is 6.

```
var merger = audioContext.createChannelMerger();
```

When connecting an input source to a channel merger, you must specify the output channel using the third argument of the connect method.

```
inputSource.connect(merger, 0, 1); /*outputs all channels of
    inputSource to right channel*/
```

▮ Merging All Channels of a Multichannel File into a Single Mono Channel

To combine a multichannel file into a single *mono* output, which is placed at the center of the stereo spectrum, you set the channel merger invocation argument to 1, and then connect the input source to the channel merger.

```
var multiChannelInputSource = audioContext.createBufferSource();
var merger = audioContext.createChannelMerger(1); /*Set number of
   channels*/
stereoInputSource.buffer = audioBuffer;
stereoInputSource.connect(merger);
merger.connect(audioContext.destination);
```

Using the Merger and Splitter Nodes Together

The merger and splitter nodes can be used in conjunction with one another to route specific input channels to specific output channels. The following code takes the left and right sides of a stereo input source and swaps them.

```
stereoInputSource.connect(splitter);
splitter.connect(merger, 0, 1); // input left and output right
splitter.connect(merger, 1, 0); // input right and output left
merger.connect(audioContext.destination);
```

If you connect an audio input source, such as an audio buffer source node, directly to a channel merger node, there is no reason to set the second argument of the connect method to a value other than 0. This is because the merger node has a *single* output.

```
audioBufferSource.connect(merger, 0, 1);
```

If the input of a channel merger is a channel splitter, the second argument of the connect method is the channel of the input source sent to the merger.

```
var channelSplitter = audioContext.createChannelSplitter();
var channelMerger = audioContext.createChannelMerger();
var sound = audioContext.createBufferSource();
sound.buffer = audioBuffer;
sound.connect(channelSplitter);
channelSplitter.connect(channelMerger, 0, 0); /*The left channel
   of playSound is connected to the channel merger*/
channelMerger.connect(audioContext.destination);
```

Summary

In this chapter, you learned how to apply stereo panning to audio input sources. You also learned how to work with the channel splitter and channel merger nodes. In the next chapter, you will explore how to create delay effects using the delay node.

---

18 The Delay Node

In the world of creative audio, delays are a common method used to create time-based effects. In this chapter, you will learn how to use the delay node to create the most common delay effects: echo, slap back, and ping-pong.

▮▮ The Delay Node

The delay node is used to adjust the time between when an input source plays and when it becomes audible. The following example connects an audio buffer to a delay node. The `delayTime.value` property determines the delay time in seconds.

```
var sound = audioContext.createBufferSource();
var delay = audioContext.createDelay();
delay.delayTime.value = 1; // One second
sound.buffer = audioBuffer;
sound.connect(delay);
delay.connect(audioContext.destination);
sound.start(audioContext.currentTime);
```

If you listen to the result of the previous example, you will notice that it does not provide the repetitive echo delay effect that is typical of an effects processor.

This is because the only thing the delay node does is pause the audio from playing for a set amount of time. If you want a repetitive echo effect, you must create it.

▌▌ Creating Echo Effects

To create an echo effect, you configure a node graph scheme that sets the delayed signal to feed back on itself.

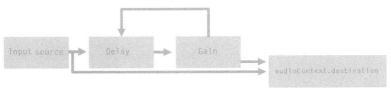

The `gain.value` property controls the amount of the effect and the `delayTime.value` property controls the length of the delay. The following code applies the effect to an audio buffer.

```
var sound = audioContext.createBufferSource();
var delayAmount = audioContext.createGain();
var delay = audioContext.createDelay();
sound.buffer = audioBuffer;
delay.delayTime.value = 0.5;
delayAmount.gain.value = 0.5;
sound.connect(delay);
delay.connect(delayAmount);
delayAmount.connect(delay);
delayAmount.connect(audioContext.destination);
sound.connect(audioContext.destination);
sound.start(audioContext.currentTime);
```

▌▌ Creating Slap Back Effects

A slap back effect is a quick delay of 40–140 ms. To create this type of effect, you split an input source and connect one branch to the delay and the other branch to the destination. You also connect the delay node to a gain node to control the volume of the effect. The node configuration for a slap back is shown in the following example and figure.

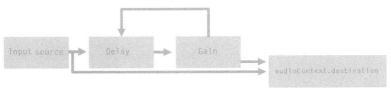

```
var sound = audioContext.createBufferSource();
var delayAmount = audioContext.createGain();
var delay = audioContext.createDelay();
sound.buffer = audioBuffer;
delay.delayTime.value = 0.06;
delayAmount.gain.value = 0.5;
sound.connect(delay);
delay.connect(delayAmount);
```

```
delayAmount.connect(audioContext.destination);
sound.connect(audioContext.destination);
sound.start(audioContext.currentTime);
```

▊ Creating a Ping-Pong Delay

A ping-pong effect is an echo delay where the echo toggles between the left and right side of the stereo spectrum. This effect can be created by spitting an input source to the left and right outputs, running each of those outputs through independent delay and gain nodes, and then feeding back the signal from the gain to its own delay as well as the delay being used to process the other side of the stereo spectrum.

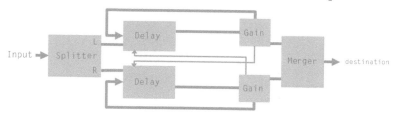

The following code implements the configuration shown in the above figure.

```
//_____BEGIN setup

var sound = audioContext.createBufferSource();
sound.buffer = audioBuffer;

var merger = audioContext.createChannelMerger(2);
var splitter = audioContext.createChannelSplitter(2);

var leftDelay = audioContext.createDelay();
var rightDelay = audioContext.createDelay();

var leftFeedback = audioContext.createGain();
var rightFeedback = audioContext.createGain();

//_____END setup

sound.connect(splitter);
sound.connect(audioContext.destination);

splitter.connect(leftDelay, 0);
leftDelay.delayTime.value = 0.5;

leftDelay.connect(leftFeedback);
leftFeedback.gain.value = 0.6;
leftFeedback.connect(rightDelay);

splitter.connect(rightDelay, 1);
rightDelay.delayTime.value = 0.5;
rightFeedback.gain.value = 0.6;

rightDelay.connect(rightFeedback);
rightFeedback.connect(leftDelay);
```

```
leftFeedback.connect(merger, 0, 0);
rightFeedback.connect(merger, 0, 1);

//_____BEGIN output

merger.connect(audioContext.destination);
//_____END output

sound.start(audioContext.currentTime);
```

▋ Summary

The delay node by itself is not complicated or difficult to use, but when combined with other nodes it can be a powerful tool for the creation of interesting audio effects. In the next chapter, you will continue exploring the node graph and learn how to apply dynamic range compression to audio input sources.

19 Dynamic Range Compression

In this chapter, you will learn about the dynamics compressor node. This node allows you to apply dynamic range compression to audio input sources.

The Dynamics Compressor Node

Dynamic range compression is the process of automatically attenuating an audio signal when its decibel level exceeds a specified threshold. This is analogous to manually turning down the volume knob on your radio when a piece of music gets too loud and then turning it back up during a quieter passage. When this action is done with a dynamic range compressor, you get the benefits of automation, speed, and the precision of a computer.

The Web Audio API comes with a built-in tool called the dynamics compressor node that allows you to apply dynamic range compression to audio input sources. To use it, you must first invoke the `createDynamicsCompressor()` method and store the resulting object in a variable.

```
var compressor = audioContext.createDynamicsCompressor();
```

The object provides you with a collection of five properties that affect the dynamic range of an audio input source. A sixth property called `reduction` is also available, but it does not affect the input source in any way. The reduction property is used exclusively to output a reduction value. These properties are briefly described in the following chart. All properties except `reduction` take a number as their assignment. The `reduction` property provides only a readout value.

Property	Description
Threshold	The decibel value above which the compression will start taking effect. Its default value is −24, with a nominal range of −100 to 0.
Ratio	Determines how much compression is administered. Setting the ratio to 2 means that for every 2 dB that the signal exceeds the threshold there will be only 1 dB in amplitude change. The ratio property takes a number between 1 and 20.
Knee	A decibel value representing the range above the threshold where a curve is created that smoothly transitions to the compressed part of the signal. Its default value is 30, with a nominal range of 0–40.
Release	Sets the release speed of the compression effect. The amount of time (in seconds) to reduce the gain by 10 dB. Its default value is 0.003, with a nominal range of 0–1.
Attack	Sets the attack speed of the compression effect. The amount of time (in seconds) to increase the gain by 10 dB. Its default value is 0.250, with a nominal range of 0 to 1.
Reduction	A numeric readout of the reduction being applied. The reduction property does not affect the signal and is used for metering purposes.

The following code demonstrates how to apply the dynamics compressor node to an audio input source. In this example, for every 12 dB the signal surpasses a threshold of −40 dB, its output is increased by 1 dB.

```
//_____BEGIN setup

  var sound = audioContext.createBufferSource();
  var compressor = audioContext.createDynamicsCompressor();
  sound.buffer = audioBuffer;

//_____END setup

  sound.connect(compressor);
  compressor.threshold.value = -40;
  compressor.ratio.value = 12;

//_____BEGIN output
  compressor.connect(audioContext.destination);
//_____END output
  sound.start(audioContext.currentTime);
```

Anyone familiar with the world of creative audio will immediately be familiar with every property available to the dynamics compressor node *except one*: `reduction`. The `reduction` property, specific to the Web Audio API, outputs a numeric value representing the amount of reduction the compressor is imposing on the input source. The following code uses `setInterval()` to allow you to see the change in reduction value as an audio input source is compressed.

```
//_____BEGIN setup
    var compressor = audioContext.createDynamicsCompressor();

    var sound = audioContext.createBufferSource();
    sound.buffer = audioBuffer;

//_____END setup

    sound.connect(compressor);
    compressor.threshold.value = -40;
    compressor.ratio.value = 12;

    //_____BEGIN output
    compressor.connect(audioContext.destination);
    //_____END output

    sound.start(audioContext.currentTime);

    window.setInterval(function() {
      console.log(compressor.reduction.value);
    }, 50);
```

▌ Summary

Using the dynamics compressor node is not complicated. It contains all the basic parameters needed to modify the dynamic range of any input source connected to it.

In the next chapter you will learn how to work with time in the Web Audio API.

20 Time

In this chapter, you will learn how to work with time to schedule Web Audio API sound playback points, how to create loops, and how to automate parameter changes.

▌▌ The Timing Clock

When you invoke a new instance of the audio context, the Web Audio API's internal timing clock begins to tick. This timing reference is in *seconds* and is expressed as a decimal number. The timing clock is tied to your computer's internal audio hardware subsystem, giving it a degree of precision that can align with sounds at the sample level. If you want to see the current value of the audio clock, you can use the currentTime property of the audio context.

```
console.log(audioContext.currentTime);
```

When you play an audio event, the Web Audio API requires you to *schedule* it. Remember that the unit you use for time value scheduling is *seconds*. If you want to schedule an event immediately, you can use the currentTime property of the audio context.

You have already had some exposure to scheduling the playback of sounds in previous chapters, such as in the following example code:

```
sound.start(audioContext.currentTime); // Play immediately
sound.start(audioContext.currentTime + 2); /*Play audio buffer two
  seconds into the future*/
```

The start Method

The start method is used to begin a sound playing. The start method takes three arguments. The first argument schedules when the sound plays, either immediately or in the future. The second argument sets a start point that determines where to begin playback from in the audio buffer. The third argument sets when a sound ceases to play. For a real-world example, imagine you were playing back a 4/4 drum loop and 0.5 seconds into the loop the drummer hit the snare drum. If you want to start playback from this point, you set the second argument of start() to 0.5.

```
sound.start(audioContext.currentTime,0.5);
```

The third argument sets how much of the sound will play. If you have a sound that is 4 seconds long and you only want to hear the first 2 seconds, then you set the third argument to 2.

```
sound.start(audioContext.currentTime,0, 2);
```

Looping Sounds

To loop sounds, you set the loop property of an audio buffer source node to true. To set the start point of a loop, you use the property loopStart. To set the end point of a loop, you use the property loopEnd.

```
sound.loop = true;
  sound.loopStart = 1; /*Set loop point at one second after
    beginning of playback*/
  sound.loopEnd = 2; /*Set loop end point at two seconds after
    beginning of playback*/
```

Sometimes when trying to discern playback and loop points, it is useful to know the length of an audio file. You can get this information using a property of the sound buffer named duration.

```
var sound = audioContext.createBufferSource();
sound.buffer = buffer;
sound.buffer.duration; // length in seconds of audio file
```

Included in the code examples for this chapter is an application that allows you to modify the playback and loop points of an audio file in real time using interactive sliders.

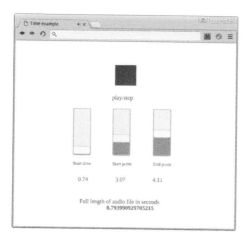

Update Your Audio Loader Library

The play() method of your audio loader library is not designed to access the second and third arguments of the start method. You can make these arguments available with the following modifications to your code:

```
soundObj.play = function(time, setStart, setDuration) {
  playSound = audioContext.createBufferSource();
  playSound.buffer = soundObj.soundToPlay;
  playSound.connect(audioContext.destination);
  playSound.start(audioContext.currentTime + time || audioContext.
    currentTime, setStart || 0, setDuration || soundObj.soundToPlay.
    duration);
};
```

The start and end point settings are now available.

```
sounds.snare.play(0, 1, 3);
```

Changing Audio Parameters over Time

Up to this point you have changed audio parameters by directly setting the value property to a number.

```
var osc = audioContext.createOscillator();
osc.frequency.value = 300;
```

The Web Audio API comes with a collection of methods that allow you to schedule audio parameter values immediately or at some point in the future. The following code shows a list of these methods.

```
setValueAtTime(arg1,arg2)
exponentialRampToValueAtTime(arg1,arg2)
linearRampToValueAtTime(arg1,arg2)
```

```
setTargetAtTime(arg1,arg2,arg3)
setValueCurveAtTime(arg1,arg2,arg3)
```

You can use these methods in place of setting the value property of an audio parameter.

```
osc.frequency.value = 100; // Set value directly
osc.frequency.setValueAtTime(arg1,arg2); /*Set value with audio
  parameter method*/
```

The Audio Parameter Methods

The setValueAtTime Method

The setValueAtTime method allows you to create an abrupt change of an audio parameter at a future period in time. The first argument is the value the parameter will be changed to, and the second argument is the time that it will take to change to that value. In the following example, 5 seconds after the code is run, a gain node parameter value is abruptly changed from 1 to 0.1.

```
var osc = audioContext.createOscillator();
var volume = audioContext.createGain();
osc.connect(volume);
volume.gain.value = 1;
volume.gain.setValueAtTime(0.1,audioContext.currentTime + 5);
osc.start(audioContext.currentTime);
volume.connect(audioContext.destination);
```

To use any of the other audio parameter methods that are described next, you must first initialize their settings using setValueAtTime(). This is shown in the code examples for each method.

The exponentialRampToValueAtTime Method

The exponentialRampToValueAtTime() method allows you to create a gradual change of the parameter value. Unlike the abrupt change of setValueAtTime(), this method follows an exponential curve. The following code demonstrates this by changing an oscillator's frequency from 200 Hz to 3 kHz over the course of 3 seconds.

```
var osc = audioContext.createOscillator();
var volume = audioContext.createGain();
osc.frequency.value = 200;
osc.frequency.setValueAtTime(osc.frequency.value, audioContext.
  currentTime); //____Set initial values!
osc.frequency.exponentialRampToValueAtTime(3000, audioContext.
  currentTime + 3);
osc.start(audioContext.currentTime);
osc.connect(audioContext.destination);
```

The `linearRampToValueAtTime` Method

The `linearRampToValueAtTime` method is similar to `exponential-RampToValueAtTime()` but follows a gradual *linear* curve instead of an exponential curve.

```
var osc = audioContext.createOscillator();
var volume = audioContext.createGain();
osc.frequency.value = 200;
osc.frequency.setValueAtTime(osc.frequency.value, audioContext.
  currentTime); // Set initial values
osc.frequency.linearRampToValueAtTime(3000, audioContext.
  currentTime + 3);
osc.start(audioContext.currentTime);
osc.connect(audioContext.destination);
```

The `setTargetAtTime()` Method

The `setTargetAtTime()` method takes three arguments. The first argument is the *final* value of the audio parameter, the second argument is the time the change will *begin*, and the third argument is a time constant that determines *how long* the change will take to complete. The larger the number of the third argument, the longer the change takes to complete.

```
var osc = audioContext.createOscillator();
var volume = audioContext.createGain();
osc.frequency.value = 200;
osc.frequency.setValueAtTime(osc.frequency.value, audioContext.
  currentTime); // Set initial values
osc.frequency.setTargetAtTime(3000, audioContext.currentTime,2);
osc.start(audioContext.currentTime);
osc.connect(audioContext.destination);
```

The `setValueCurveAtTime()` Method

The `setValueCurveAtTime()` method allows you to create a custom curve based on a collection of audio parameter values stored in an array. This method takes three arguments. The first argument is an array of values. The array used is a special kind of array called a `float32Array()`, which is a *typed* array. Typed arrays are better performing than conventional arrays and allow some Web Audio APIs to work directly with binary data. The syntax for a `float32Array()` requires you to explicitly set the number of index values and looks like the following code:

```
var waveArray = new Float32Array(10); //__Set number of index values
waveArray[0] = 20;
waveArray[1] = 200;
waveArray[2] = 20;
waveArray[3] = 200;
waveArray[4] = 20;
waveArray[5] = 200;
```

```
waveArray[6] = 20;
waveArray[7] = 200;
waveArray[8] = 20;
waveArray[9] = 200;
```

The second argument represents when you want the changes to begin, and the third argument is the time span you want the changes to take place within. The following code demonstrates this by toggling the frequency of an oscillator from 100 to 500 Hz and back again over the course of 3 seconds. This creates a *wobble* effect.

```
var waveArray = new Float32Array(10);
waveArray[0] = 100;
waveArray[1] = 500;
waveArray[2] = 100;
waveArray[3] = 500;
waveArray[4] = 100;
waveArray[5] = 500;
waveArray[6] = 100;
waveArray[7] = 500;
waveArray[8] = 100;
waveArray[9] = 500;

var osc = audioContext.createOscillator();
var volume = audioContext.createGain();
osc.frequency.value = 500;
osc.frequency.setValueAtTime(osc.frequency.value, audioContext.
  currentTime); // Set initial values
osc.frequency.setValueCurveAtTime(waveArray, audioContext.
  currentTime + 1, 3);
osc.start(audioContext.currentTime);
osc.connect(audioContext.destination);
```

▍▌ Summary

In this chapter, you learned the fundamentals of working with time. You learned how to loop and schedule sound playback, as well as how to schedule parameter value changes. In the next chapter, you will learn how to create audio visualizations using the Analyser node.

21 Creating Audio Visualizations

In this chapter, you will learn how to use the `Analyser` node to create a spectrum analyzer that displays real-time amplitude information of audio signals across a collection of frequency bands. The Web Audio API includes a node named `Analyser` that gives you real-time frequency and time domain information about audio input sources. This information can be used to create custom visual representations of audio signals that include (but are not limited to) spectrum analyzers, phase scopes, and waveform renders.

▌ A Brief Word on Fourier Analysis

Before you get started, you must first have a basic conceptual understanding of Fourier analysis. Fourier analysis is a difficult topic involving a lot of impressive math, so a proper coverage of the topic is *well* beyond the scope of this book. The main point you need to understand is that Fourier analysis is a way to take amazingly complex things like sound waves and simplify them. With this approach, a signal (referred to as a function) can be either represented or approximated by a combination of simpler periodic signals or functions, such as sine and cosine waves. Replicating a sound is also theoretically possible by *combining* an infinite number of these waveforms. In theory, a perfect replica (or perfect separation of constituent parts) is realized from this combination, but in practice, human beings lack infinite time and computing power, so you will always have to make do with an approximation.

Some of the most common forms of Fourier analysis in audio processing are called *fast Fourier transforms*, or more commonly FFTs. The goal of an FFT is to quickly give you a useful approximation without doing too much computational work and slowing down the system.

A Brief Explanation of Binary-Coded Decimal Numbers

To better understand how the Web Audio API gives you access to the time and frequency domain of audio input sources, you need to understand how to read binary-coded decimal numbers. A binary system is composed of a series of *on* and *off* values called bits. Bits are read in 8-bit groupings called bytes, which have an equivalent decimal value. Bits are read from right to left and each value is either an *on* value represented by a 1, or an *off* value represented by a 0. The decimal equivalent of a grouping of bits is calculated by exponentially counting from right to left and adding all of the *on* values together.

```
Byte:      00001001
                 ↓     ↓
Decimal:        8 + 1  =  9
```

When all bits are *on*, a byte has a value of 255. This allows for 256 total possible values (0–255).

```
1  1  1  1  1  1  1  1
128 + 64 + 32 + 16 + 8 + 4 + 2 + 1

        Total:  255

     (256 possible decimal values)
```

The Spectrum Analyzer

The following program creates a basic frequency spectrum analyzer using an oscillator as its input source. The rest of this chapter is dedicated to explaining how this code works.

JavaScript/JQuery

```
"use strict";
$(function() {
  var audioContext = new AudioContext();
  var analyzer = audioContext.createAnalyser();
  var osc = audioContext.createOscillator();
```

```javascript
    var frequencyData = new Uint8Array(analyzer.frequencyBinCount);
      //___Create array
    analyzer.getByteFrequencyData(frequencyData);
      //_____Store frequency data
    console.log(frequencyData.length);
    console.log(frequencyData);

    var app = $(".app");
    var bars = undefined;

    osc.frequency.value = 120;
    osc.connect(analyzer);
    analyzer.connect(audioContext.destination);
    osc.start(audioContext.currentTime);
    analyzer.fftSize = 2048;
    console.log(analyzer.frequencyBinCount); // 1024

    //_____BEGIN Visualization

    $(".bin-count-number").text(analyzer.fftSize / 2); // _____Bin count

    for (var i = 0; i < analyzer.frequencyBinCount; i++) {

      $(".app").append("<div></div> <span>" + i + "</span>");
    }

    bars = $(".app > div");

    function update() {
      requestAnimationFrame(update);

      analyzer.getByteFrequencyData(frequencyData);

      for (var i = 0; i < bars.length; i += 1) {

        bars[i].style.height = frequencyData[i] + 'px';

      }

    }

    update();

    //_____END visualization

});
```

HTML

```html
<!DOCTYPE html>
<html>
  <head>
    <meta charset="UTF-8">
    <title></title>
    <script type="text/javascript" src="js/jquery.js"></script>
    <script src="js/app.js"></script>
    <link rel="stylesheet" href="css/app.css" type="text/css">
  </head>
```

```
<!--_____BEGIN
  APP-->

<body>
  <p class="bin-count">
    Bin count:<b class="bin-count-number"></b>
  </p>

  <div class="app">
  </div>
</body>
<!--_____END
  APP-->
</html>
```

CSS

```
.app{

  position: relative;
  margin: 10px;

}

.app > div {
  width: 0.1px;
  background-color: orange;
  display: inline-block;
  outline-style:solid;
  outline-color:orange;
  outline-width: 0.1px;
  margin-left:8px;

}

span{
  display:inline-block;
  font-size:14px;
  color:rgba(128, 128, 128, 0.5);
  margin:2px;

}

.bin-count{
  position:absolute;
  left:30%;
  float:right;
  font-size:2em;
  height:50px;

}
```

The output of the application looks like the following figure.

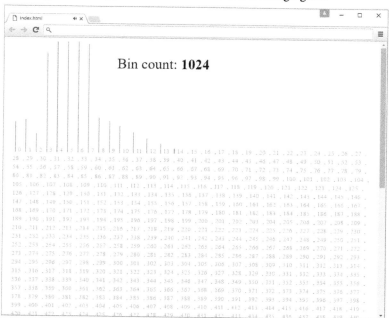

Walking through the Code

The first step to creating a spectrum analyzer is to invoke `Analyser()` and connect input sources to the returned object. For this application, the only input source used is an `oscillator` and the output of the `analyser` variable is connected directly to `audioContext.destination`.

```
var analyzer = audioContext.createAnalyser();
var oscillator = audioContext.createOscillator90;
oscillator.connect(analyzer);
analyzer.connect(audioContext.destination);
```

The `Analyser` interface enables you to perform various FFTs on the audio stream. The FFT used to create a spectrum analyzer transforms the time domain of the audio signal into normalized (or limited) frequency-domain data. This is done by chopping the original audio signal into parts, typically called *bins*, and performing an analysis and transformation on each part.

The size of the FFT is stored in the `fftSize` property of the `Analyser` node and the default value is 2048. The allowed values are any power of 2 between 32 and 2048. If you set it wrong, you will get an error. The number of bins available is one half of the `fftSize` property and is accessible by a read-only property of the `Analyser` node named `frequencyBinCount`.

```
analyzer.fftSize = 2048;
console.log(analyzer.frequencyBinCount); // 1024... or half of fftSize
```

Each bin is designated a range of frequencies called a *band*, and the following formula determines the range of each band:

$$(Sample\ Rate)/(FFT\ Size) = (Band\ Size)$$

Example:

$$44,100/2048 = 21.533203125$$

Storing the Frequency Data in an Array

The next step is to create an array to store the frequency data. A special kind of array called a *typed* array is required for this task. A typed array is an array-like object specifically designed for working with binary data.

```
//_____Create typed array
var frequencyData = new Uint8Array(analyzer.frequencyBinCount);

//_____Store frequency data
analyzer.getByteFrequencyData(frequencyData);
```

There are two kinds of typed arrays that the `Analyser` node is designed to work with: `Float32Array` and `Uint8Array`. The index values of a `Float32Array` are always a decimal number between 0 and 1. The index values of a `Uint8Array` are limited to 8 bits of information and will always be an integer between 0 and 255. Using a `Float32Array` allows for up to 32 bits of information and gives you more precision but is more resource intensive. This is in contrast to `Uint8Array`, which is more resource efficient but less precise. This application uses a `Uint8Array`. A `Float32Array` or `Uint8Array` must be created using the keyword new.

In the following code, the `Uint8Array` is invoked with a single argument that determines the number of indexes it will have by using `analyzer.frequencyBinCount`.

```
var frequencyData = new Uint8Array(analyzer.frequencyBinCount);
console.log(frequencyData.length); // 1024
```

You now store the frequency domain data in the array using `getByteFrequencyData()`.

```
analyzer.getByteFrequencyData(frequencyData);
```

If the `frequencyData` array is a `Float32Array` instead of a `Uint8Array`, you use the `getFloatFrequencyData()` method and the code looks like this:

```
analyzer.getFloatFrequencyData(frequencyData);
```

■ How to *Think About* the `frequencyData` Array

Each index value of the `frequencyData` array can be any number between 0 and 255. This value is correlated with the energy intensity of the frequency band that is designated by that particular array index. The following diagrams can help to clarify this.

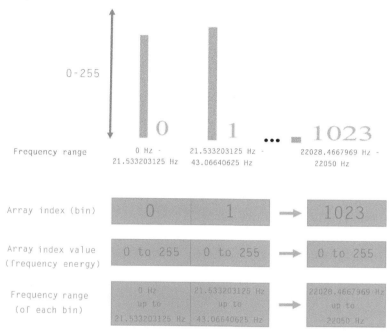

Building the Display Interface

The following line of code renders the current number of bins to the Document Object Model (DOM).

```
$(".bin-count-number").text(analyzer.fftSize / 2); //____Bin count
```

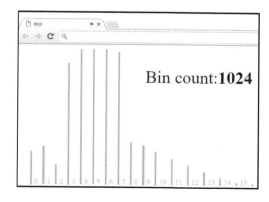

The following `for` loop creates a `div` for each bin. Inside each `div`, a `span` is created that displays a number that corresponds to each bin.

```
for (var i = 0; i < analyzer.frequencyBinCount; i++) {

  $(".app").append("<div></div> <span>" + i + "</span>");

}
```

The `bars` variable selects all `div` elements and is used later in the code.

```
bars = $(".app > div");
```

▌ Connecting the Analyzer to the DOM

To read and use `frequencyData`, the program must continuously check its current state so that the DOM can be updated with the new information. This can be done by placing `analyzer.getByteFrequencyData(frequencyData)` in the `requestAnimationFrame` function. `requestAnimationFrame` is a method that tells the browser that you wish to perform an animation. When it is time to update the animation, `requestAnimationFrame` calls the function that you passed to it. The update rate matches the display refresh rate of the web browser.

```
function update() {
  requestAnimationFrame(update);
  analyzer.getByteFrequencyData(frequencyData);

}

update();
```

To create the vertical frequency bars, the `for` loop updates the CSS height property of each `div` stored in the `bar` variable. The value given to each `div` is a pixel representation of the current `frequencyData` array index. This value is between 0 and 255 px.

```
function update() {
  requestAnimationFrame(update);
  analyzer.getByteFrequencyData(frequencyData);

  for (var i = 0; i < bars.length; i += 1) {

    bars[i].style.height = frequencyData[i] + 'px';

  }

}
update();
```

The user interface of the spectrum analyzer is designed to create a `div` for *all* bins. You can change the size of the FFT to lower the bin count.

```
analyzer.fftSize = 64;
```

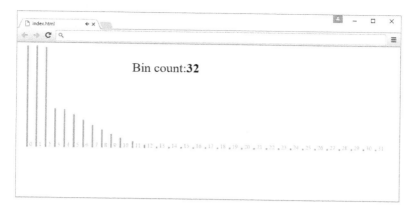

The application you created in this chapter works with frequency-domain data. If you want to work with time-domain data, the `Analyser` node has two methods that let you copy it to a typed array. The first method is `getByteTime DomainData ()` and is for use with a `Uint8Array()`. The second method is `getFloatTimeDomainData ()` and is for use with `Float32Array()`. To store the time domain data in a `Uint8Array()`, you write the following code:

```
var frequencyData = new Uint8Array(analyzer.frequencyBinCount);
analyzer.getByteTimeDomainData(frequencyData);
```

▮▮ Summary

In this chapter, you learned about the `Analyser` node and created a frequency spectrum analyzer application.

Up until now, when adding new nodes that affect audio buffers, you have applied the changes to a single node graph that affects *all* audio buffer input sources. In the next chapter, you will update the audio loader library that you created in Chapter 13 to allow users to create customized node graphs for *individual* audio buffers.

22 Adding Flexibility to the Audio Loader Abstraction

In this chapter, you will add flexibility to the audio loader abstraction and give users independently customizable node graphs for audio buffer input sources. In its current state, the audio loader library you created in Chapter 13 only allows you to create one universal node graph configuration. So any files that you load have to conform to this configuration. This is undesirable for two reasons. The first is that when you create a library, you don't want the user to have to modify its internals to get the functionality they want. The second reason is that it is useful to have the choice to apply completely different effects to different audio input sources, which requires node configurations that are independently customizable.

■ The Updated Interface

When you create any library or abstraction, it is helpful to first define what the interface will look like and then work backward toward its creation. In this case, the following example shows how the final interface will look. This is similar to the current library except that the object that `audioBatchLoader` takes as an argument has a method that defines a custom node graph. This node graph is applied to all audio files referenced as properties in the containing object.

```
"use strict";

var soundData = {
  kick: "sounds/kick.mp3",
  snare: "sounds/snare.mp3",
  //_____BEGIN custom node graph
  nodeGraph: function nodeGraph(sound) {
    var gain = audioContext.createGain();
    gain.gain.value = 1;
    sound.connect(gain);
    gain.connect(audioContext.destination);
  }
  //_____END custom node graph
}

var sound = audioBatchLoader(soundData); //Takes the object as
  argument
sound.kick.play(); // Sound plays using custom node graph
sound.snare.play(); // Sound plays using custom node graph
```

This interface allows you to add *one* method to the object; and this method then sets the node graph configuration for all sound files referenced as properties of that object.

Modifying the Library

Make a copy of the empty template folder you created in Chapter 1 and rename it to Chapter 22. In the js folder, place a copy of the completed audio loader library you modified in Chapter 20 and reference it from the index.html file.

```
<head>
  <meta charset="UTF-8">
  <title>app</title>
  <script src="js/audiolib.js"></script>
  <script src="js/app.js"></script>
  <link rel="stylesheet" href="css/app.css">
</head>
```

Next, create a directory named "sounds" and place an MP3 file named "snare" in it (this file is available in the downloadable code examples). Copy the following code into the app.js file.

```
"use strict";
var sound = audioFileLoader("sounds/snare.mp3", function(sound){
  var gain = audioContext.createGain();
  gain.gain.value = 0.2;
  sound.connect(gain);
  gain.connect(audioContext.destination);

});

window.addEventListener("mousedown", function() {
  sound.play();

});
```

```
window.addEventListener("mouseup", function() {
    sound.stop();
});
```

If you run the previous code, it will not work. In the audiolib.js file you will now modify the function named audioFileLoader so that the previous code works. These modifications will let users load *single* files, each of which has a unique node graph. Once this works, we will go over how to modify audio-BatchLoader to load *multiple* files.

In your audiolib.js file, modify the code to include a callback function like the following example:

```
var audioContext = new AudioContext();
function audioFileLoader(fileDirectory, callback) {
    var playSound = undefined;
    var soundObj = {};

    soundObj.fileDirectory = fileDirectory;
    var getSound = new XMLHttpRequest();
    getSound.open("GET", soundObj.fileDirectory, true);
    getSound.responseType = "arraybuffer";
    getSound.onload = function() {
        audioContext.decodeAudioData(getSound.response, function(buffer) {
            soundObj.soundToPlay = buffer;

        });
    }

    getSound.send();

    soundObj.play = function(time) {
        playSound = audioContext.createBufferSource();
        playSound.buffer = soundObj.soundToPlay;
        playSound.connect(audioContext.destination);
        playSound.start(audioContext.currentTime + time ||
            audioContext.currentTime, setStart || 0, setDuration ||
            soundObj.soundToPlay.duration);
        callback(playSound);

    }

    soundObj.stop = function(time) {

        playSound.stop(audioContext.currentTime + time || audioContext.
            currentTime);

    }
    return soundObj;
};
```

In the previous code, the callback now fulfills the role of a customizable node graph and the code will now work. However, there is still one problem: If the user does not use a callback, then an error results.

```
var sound = audioFileLoader("sounds/snare.mp3"); // ERROR!
```

This error can be dealt with by simply using a conditional to check if the callback is a function. If the conditional returns false (because the user didn't set it), a default node graph is set in its place.

To do this, modify the code as follows:

```
soundObj.play = function(time) {
  playSound = audioContext.createBufferSource();
  playSound.buffer = soundObj.soundToPlay;
  playSound.start(audioContext.currentTime + time || audioContext.
    currentTime);

  callback(playSound);
  if (typeof callback === "function") {
    return callback(playSound);
  }else {
    return playSound.connect(audioContext.destination);
  }

}
```

This code now works whether the function is invoked with a callback or not.

Modifying audioBatchLoader

You will now edit the audioBatchLoader function to check if its parameter object contains a method, and if it does, the method is set as the callback of audioFileLoader. This code applies a custom node graph to a group of files.

```
function audioBatchLoader(obj) {
  var callback = undefined;
  var prop = undefined;

  for (prop in obj) {
    if (typeof obj[prop] === "function") {
      callback = obj[prop];
      delete obj[prop];
    }
  }

  for (prop in obj) {

    obj[prop] = audioFileLoader(obj[prop], callback);
    //___Place function as callback

  }
  return obj;
}
```

An Explanation of the Previous Code Edit

If a method is found on obj, it is assigned to the variable named callback. The method is then deleted from obj using the delete keyword. The deletion is necessary so that the audioFileLoader does not attempt to reference it as an audio file directory.

The following code is an example of loading a collection of files with a custom node graph. This code now works.

```javascript
"use strict";

var sound = audioBatchLoader({
  snare: "sounds/snare.mp3",
  kick: "sounds/kick.mp3",
  hihat: "sounds/hihat.mp3",
  nodes: function(sound) {
    var gain = audioContext.createGain();
    sound.connect(gain);
    gain.gain.value = 0.5;
    gain.connect(audioContext.destination);

  }
});

window.addEventListener("mousedown", function() {
  sound.snare.play();
});

window.addEventListener("mouseup", function() {
  sound.snare.stop();
});
```

One thing you should be aware of is that the object that the audioBatchLoader takes as an argument is intended to have only one method. If it has more than one method, then one of them is overwritten. When using a for-in loop, the properties and methods of the targeted object are not returned in any particular order. Because of this, you cannot know which method is used and which one is overwritten until the sound is played back. For this reason, you might want to write an error check to throw an error for argument objects that have more than one method. This is left up to you to implement.

▌ Summary

In this chapter, you added additional flexibility to your audio loader library and in the process you were exposed to a real-world example of how callback functions can be useful when designing a library. In the next chapter you will learn how to build an interactive music sequencer.

23 Building a Step Sequencer

Music applications, like sequencers and drum machines, allow users to record, edit, and play back sounds as a collection of organized note arrangements. Due to the nature of the Web Audio API and its relationship to the DOM, music sequencing applications are a challenge to create. In this chapter, you will learn why this is so and how to meet the challenge by building a basic drum pattern step sequencer.

▌▌ The Problem

The Web Audio API lets you schedule events immediately or in the future. A problem with this approach is that once an event is scheduled, it cannot be unscheduled. So for example, the following code schedules three drum sounds to play in an 8th note pattern for four bars.

```
var kick = audioFileLoader("sounds/kick.mp3");
var snare = audioFileLoader("sounds/snare.mp3");
var hihat = audioFileLoader("sounds/hihat.mp3");

var tempo = 120; //_____BPM (beats per minute)
var eighthNoteTime = (60 / tempo) / 2;
```

```
function playDrums() {
  // Play 4 bars of the following:
  for (var bar = 0; bar < 4; bar++) {
    var time = bar * 8 * eighthNoteTime;
    // Play the bass (kick) drum on beats 1, 5
    kick.play(time);
    kick.play(time + 4 * eighthNoteTime);

    // Play the snare drum on beats 3, 7
    snare.play(time + 2 * eighthNoteTime);
    snare.play(time + 6 * eighthNoteTime);
    // Play the hi-hat every eighth note.
    for (var i = 0; i < 8; ++i) {
      hihat.play(time + i * eighthNoteTime);
    }
  }
}
```

If you want to change the tempo relationship of these sounds in the middle of the four bars, you can't. Instead, you have to wait until the sounds have completed playing. This is true of any scheduled events that you might want to change during playback. And this restriction is not relegated to just tempo changes.

▎ Can I Use `setInterval` or `setTimeout`?

You might be wondering if you can use `setInterval` or `setTimeout` to solve this problem. The following code uses `setInterval` to increment a counter at a specified beats per minute (BPM), and depending on the counter value, a particular drum sound is played. This creates a rhythmic pattern.

```
var kick = audioFileLoader("sounds/kick.mp3");
var snare = audioFileLoader("sounds/snare.mp3");
var hihat = audioFileLoader("sounds/hihat.mp3");

var tempo = 120; //_____BPM (beats per minute)
var milliseconds = 1000;
var eighthNoteTime = ((60 * milliseconds) / tempo) / 2;

var counter = 1;
window.setInterval(function() {
  if (counter === 8) {
    counter = 1;
  } else {
    counter += 1;
  }
  if (counter) {
    hihat.play();
  }
  if (counter === 3 || counter === 7) {
    snare.play();
  }
  if (counter === 1 || counter === 5) {
    kick.play();
  }

}, eighthNoteTime);
```

The problem with this approach is that both the `setTimeout` and `setInterval` methods have timings that are imprecise and unstable. There are two reasons for this. The first is that the smallest unit of time available to these methods is an integer of 1 millisecond, which is not precise enough for audio sample-level values like 44.100 kHz. The other problem is that unlike the Web Audio API timing clock, these methods can be interrupted by ancillary browser activity like page rendering and redraws. Although you might expect `setInterval` or `setTimeout` to run at every n^{th} millisecond, depending on factors outside your control, the value will likely be larger and audibly noticeable.

▊ The Solution

The solution to the problem is to create a relationship between the Web Audio API timing clock and the browser's internal `setTimeout` method to create a *look-ahead* mechanism that recursively loops and checks if events *will be* scheduled at some time in the future. If this is the case, the scheduling happens and the event(s) takes place. This gives you enough leeway to cancel events at the last moment if needed.

One thing to keep in mind is that because `setTimeout` is inherently unstable, we know that this relationship will always have an unstable aspect to it. Whether or not this approach is stable enough for your applications is for you to decide. One thing we can be certain of is that it is much more accurate than using `setInterval` or `setTimeout` on its own.

▊ How It Works

The basis for the relationship between the Web Audio API timing clock and the browser's internal `setTimeout` method is expressed in the following code:

```
var audioContext = new AudioContext();
var futureTickTime = audioContext.currentTime;
function scheduler() {
    if (futureTickTime < audioContext.currentTime + 0.1) {
        futureTickTime += 0.5; //____can be any time value. 0.5 happens
            to be a quarter note at 120 bpm
        console.log(futureTickTime);
    }
    window.setTimeout(scheduler, 0);
}
scheduler();
```

The way the previous code works is that the `setTimeout` function loops recursively, and upon each iteration, a conditional checks whether the value of `futureTickTime` is within a tenth of a second of the `audioContext.currentTime`. If this evaluates to `true` then `futureTickTime` is incremented by 0.5, which is *half a second* in "Web Audio Time." The `futureTickTime` variable remains set at this value until `audioContext.currentTime` "catches up with it" once again. Then within a tenth of a second, `futureTickTime` is incremented by a half-second into the future. This pattern continues for as long as the function is allowed to run.

Because a half-second translates to a quarter note at 120 beats per minute, the following code uses this information to create a 1/4th note timing count that is logged to the console.

```
var futureTickTime = audioContext.currentTime;
var counter = 1;
function scheduler() {
  if (futureTickTime < audioContext.currentTime + 0.1) {
    console.log("This is beat: " + counter);
    futureTickTime += 0.5; /*_____can be any time value. 0.5 happens
      to be a quarter note at 120 bpm*/

    counter += 1;
    if (counter > 4) {
      counter = 1;
    }
  }
  window.setTimeout(scheduler, 0);
}
scheduler();
```

The following code builds on the previous example and plays an oscillator on each count. The oscillator is connected to a gain node named metronomeVolume which is connected to the destination. The gain node is added because the final application in this chapter uses it to toggle the oscillator volume on and off.

```
var futureTickTime = audioContext.currentTime;
var counter = 1;
var osc = audioContext.createOscillator();
var metronomeVolume = audioContext.createGain();
function playMetronome(time) {
  osc = audioContext.createOscillator();
  osc.connect(metronomeVolume);
```

```
    metronomeVolume.connect(audioContext.destination);
    osc.start(time);
    osc.stop(time + 0.1);

}

function scheduler() {
    if (futureTickTime < audioContext.currentTime + 0.1) {

        console.log("This is beat: " + counter);
        playMetronome(futureTickTime);
        futureTickTime += 0.5; //_____can be any time value. 0.5 happens
        //_____to be a quarter note at 120 bpm

        counter += 1;
        if (counter > 4) {
            counter = 1;
        }
    }
    window.setTimeout(scheduler, 0);
}
scheduler();
```

▌ Changing Tempo

If you want to change the tempo, you have to change the time relationship between events. You can do this by altering when events are scheduled to start with the `futureTickTime` variable. The following formula is useful for converting beats (quarter notes) to seconds.

```
var tempo = 120.0; // tempo (in beats per minute);
var secondsPerBeat = (60.0 / tempo);
```

The application you build assumes the use of a 16th note grid. You can design it with any beat division(s) you want, but for simplicity it is hard-coded with 16 notes. The following code converts the `futureTickTime` variable from a time value that represents a quarter note to a time value that represents a 16th note. The oscillator is also modified to play a different frequency on the downbeat.

```
var futureTickTime = audioContext.currentTime;
var counter = 1;
var tempo = 120;
var secondsPerBeat = 60 / tempo;
var counterTimeValue = (secondsPerBeat / 4); //___16th note
var osc = audioContext.createOscillator();
var metronomeVolume = audioContext.createGain();

function playMetronome(time) {
    osc = audioContext.createOscillator();
    osc.connect(metronomeVolume);
    metronomeVolume.connect(audioContext.destination);
    osc.frequency.value = 500;
    osc.start(time);
    osc.stop(time + 0.1);

}
```

```
function scheduler() {
  if (futureTickTime < audioContext.currentTime + 0.1) {
    console.log("This is 16ᵗʰ is: " + counter);
    playMetronome(futureTickTime);
    futureTickTime += counterTimeValue;

    if (counter === 1) {
      osc.frequency.value = 500;
    } else {
      osc.frequency.value = 300;
    }

    counter += 1;
    if (counter > 16) {
      counter = 1;
    }
  }
  window.setTimeout(scheduler, 0);
}

scheduler();
```

You can now change the tempo by modifying the tempo variable.

▌ Building the Sequencer

You are now going to build the sequencer application. Create a copy of the *Web Audio template* folder you created in Chapter 1 and rename it to *sequencer*. In the *index.html* file, reference both the JQuery library and the *audiolib.js* file that you updated in Chapter 20. Inside the sequencer folder, create a folder named *sounds* and place the audio files for the sequencer application in it.

Copy the following code to *app.js* and save the file. This code refactors the previous code you have written. This version is more readable and the metronome is given its own function.

```
"use strict";
var audioContext = new AudioContext();
var futureTickTime = audioContext.currentTime,
  counter = 1,
  tempo = 120,
  secondsPerBeat = 60 / tempo,
  counterTimeValue = (secondsPerBeat / 4),
  osc = audioContext.createOscillator(),
  metronomeVolume = audioContext.createGain();

//_____BEGIN metronome
function playMetronome(time, playing) {
  if (playing) {
    osc = audioContext.createOscillator();
    osc.connect(metronomeVolume);
    metronomeVolume.connect(audioContext.destination);
    osc.frequency.value = 500;
    if (counter === 1) {
      osc.frequency.value = 500;
```

```
    } else {
      osc.frequency.value = 300;
    }
    osc.start(time);
    osc.stop(time + 0.1);
  }
}


//_____END Metronome
function playTick() {
  console.log("This is 16th note: " + counter);
  counter += 1;
  futureTickTime += counterTimeValue;
  if (counter > 16) {
    counter = 1;
  }
}


function scheduler() {
  if (futureTickTime < audioContext.currentTime + 0.1) {
    playMetronome(futureTickTime , true);
    playTick();
  }
  window.setTimeout(scheduler, 0);
}
scheduler();
```

▎▊ Playing Back Sounds in Sequence

You will now create a series of arrays that represent music sequencer *tracks*. Each of these arrays stores counter values. On each iteration of the counter, a *for* loop runs to check if any of the arrays holds the current counter value. If any of them does, the sound associated with that array plays. The arrays are associated with the correct sound through a function named scheduleSound(). This function takes four arguments:

- The track array

- The sound to play

- The current count value

- The time to schedule the sound

The track arrays are populated with values so that you can hear a drum sequence immediately.

```
var futureTickTime = audioContext.currentTime,
  counter = 1,
  tempo = 120,
  secondsPerBeat = 60 / tempo,
```

```
    counterTimeValue = (secondsPerBeat / 4),
    osc = audioContext.createOscillator(),
    metronomeVolume = audioContext.createGain();

/*_____BEGIN load sound
   samples*/

var kick = audioFileLoader("sounds/kick.mp3");
var snare = audioFileLoader("sounds/snare.mp3");
var hihat = audioFileLoader("sounds/hihat.mp3");
var shaker = audioFileLoader("sounds/shaker.mp3");

//_____END load sound samples

//_____BEGIN Array Tracks

var kickTrack = [1, 9, 11],
    snareTrack = [5, 13],
    hiHatTrack = [13, 14, 15, 16],
    shakerTrack = [1, 2, 3, 4, 5, 6, 7, 8, 9, 10, 11, 12, 13, 14, 15, 16];

//_____END Array Tracks

function scheduleSound(trackArray, sound, count, time) {

  for (var i = 0; i < trackArray.length; i += 1) {
    if (count === trackArray[i]) {
      sound.play(time);
    }
  }
}

//_____BEGIN metronome
function playMetronome(time, playing) {

  if (playing) {
    osc = audioContext.createOscillator();
    osc.connect(audioContext.destination);
    osc.frequency.value = 500;
    if (counter === 1) {
      osc.frequency.value = 500;
    } else {
      osc.frequency.value = 300;
    }
    osc.start(time);
    osc.stop(time + 0.1);
  }
}

//_____END Metronome

function playTick() {

  console.log("This is 16th note: " + counter);
  counter += 1;
  futureTickTime += counterTimeValue;
```

```
      if (counter > 16) {
        counter = 1;
      }

}

function scheduler() {
    if (futureTickTime < audioContext.currentTime + 0.1) {
      playMetronome(futureTickTime, true);

      scheduleSound(kickTrack, kick, counter, futureTickTime -
        audioContext.currentTime);
      scheduleSound(snareTrack, snare, counter, futureTickTime -
        audioContext.currentTime);
      scheduleSound(hiHatTrack, hihat, counter, futureTickTime -
        audioContext.currentTime);
      scheduleSound(shakerTrack, shaker, counter, futureTickTime -
        audioContext.currentTime);

      playTick();
    }
    window.setTimeout(scheduler, 0);
}

scheduler();
```

You might be wondering why the scheduleSound() function invocations are subtracting the audioContext.currentTime from the futureTickTime().

```
scheduleSound(kickTrack, kick, counter, futureTickTime -
  audioContext.currentTime);
```

This is done because the audio library you built in Chapter 13 is designed to reference audioContext.currentTime by default and adds any additional numeric arguments to this value. You subtract audioContext.current-Time from futureTickTime because these values will be combined when the play() method of your library is invoked.

When scheduler() is invoked, the drum sequence does not start immediately because it takes time for the audio buffers and files to load. This behavior can be corrected by modifying the code so that the scheduler is initiated by a *play/stop* button. In your HTML code, create a button with a class of play-stop-button and give it text of play/stop.

```
<!DOCTYPE html>
<html>
  <head>
    <meta charset="UTF-8">
    <title></title>
    <script src="https://ajax.googleapis.com/ajax/libs/
      jquery/2.1.0/jquery.js"></script>
    <script src="js/audiolib.js"></script>
    <script src="js/app.js"></script>
    <link rel="stylesheet" href="css/app.css">
  </head>
```

```
<!--_____BEGIN APP-->
<body>

<!--HTML code-->
<button class="play-stop-button">
  Play / Stop
</button>

</body>
<!--_____END APP-->
</html>
```

You now use JQuery to interface with the DOM and have to wrap your code in a document-ready function. The following code defines the *play/stop* button functionality.

```
$(function() {
  var futureTickTime = audioContext.currentTime,
    counter = 1,
    tempo = 120,
    secondsPerBeat = 60 / tempo,
    counterTimeValue = (secondsPerBeat / 4),
    osc = audioContext.createOscillator(),
    metronomeVolume = audioContext.createGain(),
    timerID = undefined,
    isPlaying = false;

  /*_____BEGIN load sound
    samples*/

  var kick = audioFileLoader("sounds/kick.mp3");
  var snare = audioFileLoader("sounds/snare.mp3");
  var hihat = audioFileLoader("sounds/hihat.mp3");
  var shaker = audioFileLoader("sounds/shaker.mp3");

  /*_____END load sound
    samples*/

  //_____BEGIN Array Tracks

  var kickTrack = [1, 9, 11],
    snareTrack = [5, 13],
    hiHatTrack = [13, 14, 15, 16],
    shakerTrack = [1, 2, 3, 4, 5, 6, 7, 8, 9, 10, 11, 12, 13, 14,
      15, 16];

  //_____END Array Tracks

  function scheduleSound(trackArray, sound, count, time) {

    for (var i = 0; i < trackArray.length; i += 1) {
      if (count === trackArray[i]) {
        sound.play(time);
      }
    }
  }

}
```

```
//_____BEGIN metronome

function playMetronome(time, playing) {

  if (playing) {
    osc = audioContext.createOscillator();
    osc.connect(metronomeVolume);
    metronomeVolume.connect(audioContext.destination);
    osc.frequency.value = 500;
    if (counter === 1) {
      osc.frequency.value = 500;
    } else {
      osc.frequency.value = 300;
    }
      osc.start(time);
      osc.stop(time + 0.1);
    }
  }


  //_____END Metronome

  function playTick() {
    console.log("This is 16th note: " + counter);
    counter += 1;
    futureTickTime += counterTimeValue;
    if (counter > 16) {
      counter = 1;
    }
  }


  function scheduler() {
    if (futureTickTime < audioContext.currentTime + 0.1) {
      playMetronome(futureTickTime, true);
      scheduleSound(kickTrack, kick, counter, futureTickTime -
        audioContext.currentTime);
      scheduleSound(snareTrack, snare, counter, futureTickTime -
        audioContext.currentTime);
      scheduleSound(hiHatTrack, hihat, counter, futureTickTime -
        audioContext.currentTime);
      scheduleSound(shakerTrack, shaker, counter, futureTickTime -
        audioContext.currentTime);
      playTick();
    }

    timerID = window.setTimeout(scheduler, 0);
  }
scheduler();
  function play() {
    isPlaying = !isPlaying;

    if (isPlaying) {
      counter = 1;
      futureTickTime = audioContext.currentTime;
      scheduler();
    } else {
      window.clearTimeout(timerID);
```

```
    }
  }
  $(".play-stop-button").on("click", function() {
    play();
  });
});
```

If you launch this code from your server and click the *play/start* button, it will start and stop the application.

▌▌ Creating the User Interface Grid

So far you have built a working 16th note sequencer that plays back sound sequences via a collection of "array tracks" in code. You are now going to create a user interface that allows users to create these sequences from a web page.

To do this, you create four div elements positioned as rows, and each of these contains 16 child divs. The CSS displays these child divs horizontally as a collection of small squares. The first row controls playback of the kick drum, the second row the snare, the third row the hi-hat, and the fourth row the shaker. The sequencer has an additional button that turns the metronome on and off and an input slider that controls the tempo.

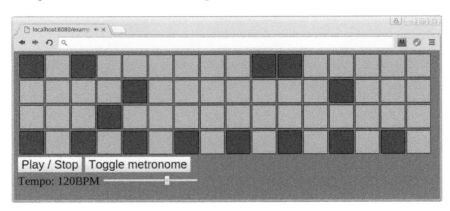

HTML

The following code is the HTML for the application.

```
<!DOCTYPE html>
<html>
  <head>
    <meta charset="UTF-8">
    <title>app</title>
    <script src="https://ajax.googleapis.com/ajax/libs/
      jquery/2.1.0/jquery.js"></script>
    <link rel="stylesheet" href="css/app.css">
```

```
    <script src="js/audiolib.js"></script>
    <script src="js/app.js"></script>

  </head>
  <!--_____BEGIN APP-->
  <body>
    <div class="app-grid">
    </div>
    <button class="play-stop-button">
    Play / Stop
    </button>
    <button class="metronome">Toggle metronome</button>
    <div id="tempoBox">Tempo: <span id="showTempo">120</span>BPM
      <input id="tempo" type="range" min="30.0" max="160.0"
      step="1" value="120" ></div>
  </body>
  <!--_____END APP-->
</html>
```

CSS

The following code is the CSS for the application.

```
body{
  background-color:red;
  font-size:25px;
}

button{
  margin-bottom:5px;
  font-size:25px;
}

.track-step{
  width:50px;
  height:50px;
  display:inline-block;
  background-color:orange;
  outline-style:solid;
  outline-width:1px;
  margin-left:5px;
}
```

To create the div elements for the grid, you use a nested JavaScript for loop. Each collection of grid items has a parent container.

```
function play() {
  isPlaying = !isPlaying;

  if (isPlaying) {
    counter = 1;
    futureTickTime = audioContext.currentTime;
    scheduler();
  } else {
    window.clearTimeout(timerID);
  }
}
```

```
//_____BEGIN create grid
  for (var i = 1; i <= 4; i += 1) {
    $(".app-grid").append("<div class='track-" + i + "-container'
      </div>");
    for (var j = 1; j < 17; j += 1) {
      $(".track-" + i + "-container").append("<div class='grid-item
        track-step step-" + j + "'</div>");
    }
  }
//_____END create grid
```

The following code allows you to toggle the metronome on and off.

```
$(".play-stop-button").on("click", function() {
  play();
});
//_____BEGIN metronome toggle
  $(".metronome").on("click", function() {
    if (metronomeVolume.gain.value) {
      metronomeVolume.gain.value = 0;
    } else {
      metronomeVolume.gain.value = 1;
    }
  });
//_____END metronome toggle
```

Next you write code that lets users control the tempo from the HTML input range slider and displays the current tempo on the web page. First, modify the playTick() function:

```
function playTick() {
  secondsPerBeat = 60 / tempo;
  counterTimeValue = (secondsPerBeat / 4);
  console.log("This is 16th note: " + counter);
  counter += 1;
  futureTickTime += counterTimeValue;
  if (counter > 16) {
    counter = 1;
  }
}
```

Then create the event listener used to control the tempo from the slider:

```
$(".metronome").on("click", function() {
  if (metronomeVolume.gain.value) {
    metronomeVolume.gain.value = 0;
  } else {
    metronomeVolume.gain.value = 1;
  }
});

$("#tempo").on("change", function() {
  tempo = this.value;
  $("#showTempo").html(tempo);
});
```

You can now modify the tempo of the sequence by moving the HTML input slider.

Adding Interactivity to the Grid Elements

Each collection of elements with a class of grid-item has a parent. The parent elements are dynamically created as shown in the following code:

```
<div class="track-1-container"></div>
<div class="track-2-container"></div>
<div class="track-3-container"></div>
<div class="track-4-container"></div>
```

JQuery has a method named index() that allows you to capture an element's index value relative to a parent element. In the case of the sequencer application, the index value of the first grid-item of each row is 0 and the last grid-item index is 15. You can give this value an offset of +1 so that the first index grid-item is referenced as 1 and the last is referenced as 16. This allows for a correlation between the grid-item index values and the counter value. You can capture this information by setting an event listener to all elements with a class of grid-item. When the user clicks the grid-item, the offset index value is either *pushed to* or *removed from* a corresponding track array dependent on whether the grid-item is *active or not*. This is what determines if a sound will play at a certain point in the music sequence. The following code implements this feature and also modifies the CSS background-color of the grid-item based on whether it is active or not.

```
//_____BEGIN create grid
for (var i = 1; i <= 4; i += 1) {
  $(".app-grid").append("<div class='track-" + i + "-container'</div>");
  for (var j = 1; j < 17; j += 1) {
    $(".track-" + i + "-container").append("<div class='grid-item
      track-step step-" + j + "'</div>");
  }
}
//_____END create grid

//_____BEGIN Grid interactivity
function sequenceGridToggler(domEle, arr) {
  $(domEle).on("mousedown", ".grid-item", function() {

    var gridIndexValue = $(this).index(); /*_____Get index
      of grid-item*/
    var offset = gridIndexValue + 1; /*_____Add +1 so
      value starts at 1 instead of 0*/
    var index = arr.indexOf(offset); /*_____Check if
      value exists in array*/

    if (index > -1) { /*_____If index of
      item exist.....*/

      arr.splice(index, 1); //_____then remove it....
      $(this).css("backgroundColor", ""); /*_____and change
        color of DOM element to default*/
```

```
        } else { /*_____If item does
          not exist.....*/
          arr.push(offset); /*_____then push it to
            track array*/
          $(this).css("background-color", "purple"); /*_and change
            color of DOM element to purple.*/


      }
    });
  }

  sequenceGridToggler(".track-1-container", kickTrack);
  sequenceGridToggler(".track-2-container", snareTrack);
  sequenceGridToggler(".track-3-container", hiHatTrack);
  sequenceGridToggler(".track-4-container", shakerTrack);
//_____END Grid interactivity
```

Now set the track arrays so that they are empty.

```
var kickTrack = [1, 9, 11],
    snareTrack = [5, 13],
    hiHatTrack = [13, 14, 15, 16],
    shakerTrack = [1, 2, 3, 4, 5, 6, 7, 8, 9, 10, 11, 12, 13,
      14, 15, 16];

var kickTrack = [ ],
    snareTrack = [ ],
    hiHatTrack = [ ],
    shakerTrack = [ ];
```

You can now run the sequencer and play back sounds by clicking the squares. The tempo also changes when the slider is moved.

▍ Summary

In this chapter, you learned how to build a basic music sequencer. You now understand the core techniques needed to build Web Audio API applications that rely on event scheduling.

24 AJAX and JSON

In this chapter, you are going to learn how to query data using web APIs and to create your own web API for accessing synth patch data to use in a web audio synthesizer. Third-party web services commonly allow a portion of their data to be accessible via a web API. This gives you the ability to query data on their server and use their data in your applications. An example is the iTunes public search API that lets developers search media titles in the iTunes store. To begin, you must first learn about two technologies: AJAX and JSON.

▌ AJAX

AJAX is an acronym that stands for *Asynchronous JavaScript and XML*. This is a technology that allows you to use JavaScript to access data asynchronously. You have already worked with AJAX in previous chapters when loading audio buffers using the XMLHttpRequest object. The X in AJAX refers to XML, which stands for Extensible Markup Language. This was originally the data exchange format used with AJAX and is rarely used now. In modern web development, the data exchange format you use is JSON.

JSON

JSON stands for *JavaScript Object Notation*, and it is a data exchange format for transmitting and receiving data over the HTTP protocol when working with web APIs. JSON objects are nearly identical to JavaScript object literals, making them easy to work with. The difference between a JSON object and a JavaScript object literal is that JSON objects are not assigned to a variable and their keys need to be written as strings. JSON objects are stored in JavaScript files. The following code is an example of a JSON object.

```
{
  "buzzFunk": [{
    "type": "sawtooth",
    "frequency": 65.25

  }, {
    "type": "triangle",
    "frequency": 65.25

  }, {

    "type": "sawtooth",
    "frequency": 67.25

  }]
}
```

Making an AJAX Call to the iTunes Search API

To demonstrate how to interact with a third-party web API, you are now going to make a query to the iTunes search API.

Make a copy of the "web audio template" folder you created in Chapter 1, rename it to "itunes api example" and drag it to the sidebar in Sublime Text. Next, reference the JQuery library from the index.html file and then copy the following code to the app.js file.

```
$(function() {
  var apiURL = "https://itunes.apple.com/search?term=funk&
    media=music&callback=?";
  $.getJSON(apiURL, function(data) {
    console.log(data);

  });
});
```

Go to Start Sublime Server and in your web browser go to localhost:8080. Open the console and you will see an object being returned.

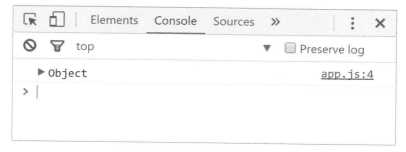

If you click the arrow and unfold the object, you will see a list of objects that each contains data.

You have just queried the iTunes search API for any music that includes the keyword "funk" and are now in possession of a JavaScript object that contains this data.

How the Code Works

JQuery has a collection of methods that abstract the `XMLHttpRequest` object and lets developers make AJAX requests with a simple syntax. One of these methods is `$.getJSON`. This method issues a request to a server that returns the queried data. The first argument of `$.getJSON` is a URL (commonly referred to as an *endpoint*). The endpoint is written as a string, and if you look closely you can see the search terms embedded in it. These are key/value pairs such as `term=funk` and `media=music`.

```
"https://itunes.apple.com/search?term=funk&media=music& callback=?";
```

The part of the endpoint after the "?" symbol is called the *query string*. This part of the URL contains the data that is being queried. The "&" symbol separates the key/value pairs.

The iTunes API search terms are assigned to specific keys and in the previous code, these are `term` and `media`. There is no standardization across web APIs for key/value names, and they are different for each web API. Because the URL structure for all web APIs is different, you will need to read the documentation for any that you are working with. The documentation for the iTunes search API is here: https://affiliate.itunes.apple.com/resources/documentation/itunes-store-web-service-search-api/.

The next part of the URL string lets you to set a callback to run once the query completes. In the code example, the callback of $.getJSON is used. If you want to make a call to the iTunes search API on page load and invoke a function on completion, it looks like the following code:

HTML

```
<!DOCTYPE html>
<html>
  <head>
    <meta charset="UTF-8">
    <title>app</title>
    <script type="text/javascript" src="https://ajax.googleapis.
      com/ajax/libs/jquery/2.1.0/jquery.js">
    </script>
    <script src="js/app.js"></script>
    <link rel="stylesheet" href="css/app.css">
  </head>
  <!--_____BEGIN APP-->
  <body>
  </body>
  <!--_____END APP-->
</html>
```

JavaScript

```
function logger(data) {
  console.log(data);
}
```

In the previous example, a function named `logger` is run when the query completes.

The $.getJSON method takes a callback as a second argument. The callback returns the data object via an argument. In the following code, this argument is named `data`, but you can name it anything you want.

```
$.getJSON(apiURL, function(data) {
  console.log(data);
});
```

Creating Your Own Web API to Reference Synthesizer Patch Data

You are now going to create your own web API. The goal of this exercise is to demonstrate how to reference a JSON object that contains synthesizer patch data. The data you will create for your web API is a collection of settings for the oscillators of a synth. The user interface of the application appears as in the figure below, and the completed code is available in the resource examples for this chapter.

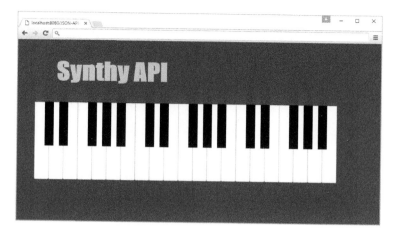

Make a new copy of the "web audio template" folder you created in Chapter 1, name the folder "synthy_api", and drag the folder to the sidebar in Sublime Text. Next, reference the JQuery library from the index.html file. Inside the "js" folder, create a new file named data.js and copy the following JSON object to it and save the file.

```
{
    "buzzFunk": [{
        "type": "sawtooth",
        "frequency": 65.25

    }, {

        "type": "triangle",
        "frequency": 65.25

    }, {

        "type": "sawtooth",
        "frequency": 67.25

    }]
}
```

In the app.js file, save the following code:

```
$(function() {
    $.getJSON("js/data.js", function(data) {
        console.log(data);
    });
});
```

Go to Start Sublime Server and in your web browser go to localhost:8080. In the Chrome console, you will see the JSON object.

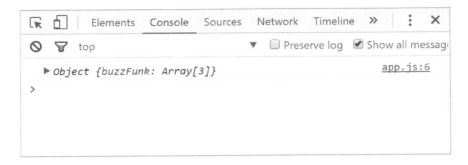

If you unfold the object, you will see its internals.

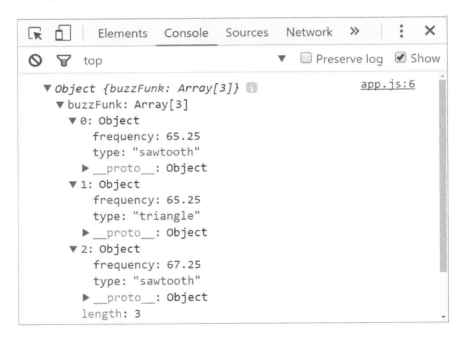

A JSON object is different from a regular JavaScript object literal because it is not assigned to a variable. However, once the data is returned, it is assigned to a variable and can be passed around and assigned to other variables.

```
$(function() {
  $.getJSON("js/data.js", function(data) {
    var patchParams = data;
    console.log(patchParams); // object
  });
});
```

24. AJAX and JSON

▐ The Data Structure

The data structure of the JSON object you are working with contains a single object property named buzzFunk, which is an array containing three objects and each holds oscillator data. When this data is loaded into your synth, all three oscillators combine to create a single sound. Each object has type and frequency settings for the oscillator that references it.

The HTML and CSS codes for the keyboard interface used to play the synth that loads the JSON data are given below. Copy the HTML code to index.html and the CSS code to app.css.

HTML

```
<body>
  <h1> Synthy API </h1>
  <ul id="piano">

    <li><div class="white-key key" id="c1"></div></li>
    <li><div class="black-key key" id="c#1"></div></li>
    <li><div class="white-key key" id="d1"></div></li>
    <li><div class="black-key key" id="d#1"></div></li>
    <li><div class="white-key key" id="e1"></div></li>
    <li><div class="white-key key" id="f1"></div></li>
    <li><div class="black-key key" id="f#1"></div></li>
    <li><div class="white-key key" id="g1"></div></li>
    <li><div class="black-key key" id="g#1"></div></li>
    <li><div class="white-key key" id="a1"></div></li>
    <li><div class="black-key key" id="b#1"></div></li>
    <li><div class="white-key key" id="b1"></div></li>
    <li><div class="white-key key" id="c2"></div></li>
    <li><div class="black-key key" id="c#2"></div></li>
    <li><div class="white-key key" id="d2"></div></li>
    <li><div class="black-key key" id="d#2"></div></li>
    <li><div class="white-key key" id="e2"></div></li>
    <li><div class="white-key key" id="f2"></div></li>
    <li><div class="black-key key" id="f#2"></div></li>
    <li><div class="white-key key" id="g2"></div></li>
    <li><div class="black-key key" id="g#2"></div></li>
    <li><div class="white-key key" id="a2"></div></li>
    <li><div class="black-key key" id="b#2"></div></li>
    <li><div class="white-key key" id="b2"></div></li>
    <li><div class="white-key key" id="c3"></div></li>
    <li><div class="black-key key" id="c#3"></div></li>
    <li><div class="white-key key" id="d3"></div></li>
    <li><div class="black-key key" id="d#3"></div></li>
    <li><div class="white-key key" id="e3"></div></li>
    <li><div class="white-key key" id="f3"></div></li>
    <li><div class="black-key key" id="f#3"></div></li>
    <li><div class="white-key key" id="g3"></div></li>
    <li><div class="black-key key" id="g#3"></div></li>
    <li><div class="white-key key" id="a3"></div></li>
    <li><div class="black-key key" id="b#3"></div></li>
    <li><div class="white-key key" id="b3"></div></li>
  </ul>

</body>
```

CSS

```css
body{
  background-color:purple;
}

h1{
  font-family:"impact";
  color:rgb(228, 208, 230);
  margin-left:10%;
  font-size:70px;
}

li {
  list-style:none;
  float:left;
  display:inline;
  width:40px;
  position:relative;
}

.white-key{
  display:block;
  height:220px;
  background:#fff;
  border:1px solid #ddd;
  border-radius:0 0 3px 3px;
}

.black-key {
  display:inline-block;
  position:absolute;
  top:0px;
  left:-12px;
  width:25px;
  height:125px;
  background:#000;
  z-index:1;

}
```

The application uses a factory function to load the JSON data. This function takes two arguments. The first argument is an endpoint that contains the JSON file, and the second is a property of the JSON object that contains the patch you want to load. Currently, the JSON file has only one patch named buzzFunk. The final loading interface for the JSON data looks like the following code:

```js
var synth = apiReader("js/data.js", "buzzFunk"); // load patch
synth.play(keyByDOMIndex); // play a specific note on keyboard
synth.stop(); // stop playing
```

Delete any code present in app.js and replace it with the following code:

```js
"use strict";
var synth = apiReader("js/data.js", "buzzFunk");
$(function() {
```

```
$(".key").on("mouseover", function() {
    var index = $(this).index('.key');
    synth.play(index);
});
$(".key").on("mouseout", function() {
    synth.stop();
});
});
```

In the "js" folder, create a new file named module.js and reference it in the index.html file between the JQuery library and app.js file.

```
<head>
    <meta charset="UTF-8">
    <title>app</title>
    <script type="text/javascript" src="https://ajax.googleapis.
        com/ajax/libs/jquery/2.1.0/jquery.js" charset="utf-8"></script>
    <script src="js/module.js"></script>
    <script src="js/app.js"></script>
    <link rel="stylesheet" href="css/app.css">
</head>
```

In module.js, copy and save the following code:

```
"use strict";
var audioContext = new AudioContext();

var apiReader = function(endpoint, patchProp) {

    $(function() {

        $.getJSON(endpoint, function(data) {
            app.patchParams = data[patchProp];
        })

    });

    var app = {

        patchParams: undefined,
        oscillators: undefined,

        play: function(id) {

            app.oscillators = app.patchParams.map(function(val) {

                var osc = audioContext.createOscillator();
                osc.type = val.type;
                osc.frequency.value = val.frequency;
                osc.detune.value = (val.frequency) + (id * 100);
                osc.connect(audioContext.destination)
                osc.start(audioContext.currentTime)

                return osc;
            });

        },
```

```
      stop: function() {
        for (var i = 0; i < app.oscillators.length; i += 1) {
          app.oscillators[i].stop(audioContext.currentTime);
        }
      }
    }

    return app;

};
```

Launch the `index.html` file from Sublime Server and hover your mouse over the synth keys. You will hear the synth play a collection of oscillators that reference the settings in the loaded patch data.

▌ How the Code Works

In the `module.js` file, the factory function named `apiReader` takes two arguments. The first argument is named `endpoint` and is the endpoint location of the JSON file. The second argument is named `patchProp` and is the property of the JSON object that contains the synth patch data. The endpoint argument value is passed to the `$.getJSON` method. In the body of the `$.getJSON` callback, the desired `patch` of the returned object is referenced and stored in a property of the app object named `app.patchParams`.

The purpose of the app object is to contain the properties and methods that *create*, *connect*, *start*, and *stop* oscillators using the settings that are listed in the JSON object property. The first method of the app object is named `play`. It takes a single argument and is the index value of a DOM element that represents a key. When the `play` method is invoked, the map method loops through each object in the `app.patchParams` array and creates an oscillator on each iteration. The `type`, `frequency.value`, and `detune.value` properties of each oscillator are assigned. The oscillator is then connected to the node graph and set to start playing.

```
app.oscillators = app.patchParams.map(function(val) {
  var osc = audioContext.createOscillator();
  osc.type = val.type;
  osc.frequency.value = val.frequency;
  osc.detune.value = (val.frequency) + (id * 100);
  osc.connect(audioContext.destination);
  osc.start(audioContext.currentTime);
  return osc;
});
```

The following code provides the index value of a DOM element (the keyboard note the user hovers their mouse over) multiplied by 100. The result is added to the oscillator frequency and assigned to the `detune.value` property. This makes the oscillators play back at half-step intervals relative to the keyboard interface.

```
osc.detune.value = (val.frequency) + (id * 100);
```

Each oscillator is then returned and stored in an array named app. oscillators.

The `stop` method is used to stop the oscillators from playing. This method loops through `app.oscillators` and invokes a Web Audio API stop method on each one.

```
stop: function() {
  for (var i = 0; i < app.oscillators.length; i += 1) {
    app.oscillators[i].stop(audioContext.currentTime);
  }
}
```

In `app.js`, the `apiReader` function is invoked, which returns an object named synth.

```
var synth = apiReader("js/data.js", "buzzFunk");
```

The `play` and `stop` methods are placed in two event listeners to start and stop the oscillators on mouse events.

```
$(".key").on("mouseover", function() {
  var index = $(this).index('.key');
  synth.play(index);
});
$(".key").on("mouseout", function() {
  synth.stop();
});
```

When the `play` method is invoked, the current index value of the `div` element (the "keyboard note") is captured and passed to the function.

```
var index = $(this).index('.key');//__get index value of key
synth.play(index);//_____pass it to play method
```

Building on the API

The code in `module.js` is designed to load only the `type` and `frequency` of oscillators, but what if you wanted to load other custom settings such as volume? The following code adds a volume setting to each oscillator.

data.js

```
{
  "buzzFunk": [{
    "type": "sawtooth",
    "frequency": 65.25,
    "volume": 1
  }, {
    "type": "triangle",
    "frequency": 65.25,
    "volume": 1
  }, {
```

```
      "type": "sawtooth",
      "frequency": 67.25,
      "volume": 0.3
  }]
}
```

module.js

```
"use strict";
var audioContext = new AudioContext();
var apiReader = function(endpoint, patchProp) {

  $(function() {

    $.getJSON(endpoint, function(data) {
      app.patchParams = data[patchProp];
    })

  });
  var app = {
    patchParams: undefined,
    gainNodes: undefined,
    oscillators: undefined,

    play: function(id) {

      app.gainNodes = app.patchParams.map(function(val) {

        var gain = audioContext.createGain();
        gain.gain.value = val.volume;
        return gain;

      });
      app.oscillators = app.patchParams.map(function(val, i) {

        var osc = audioContext.createOscillator();
        osc.type = val.type;
        osc.frequency.value = val.frequency;
        osc.detune.value = (val.frequency) + (id * 100);
        osc.connect(app.gainNodes[i]);
        app.gainNodes[i].connect(audioContext.destination);
        osc.connect(audioContext.destination);
        osc.start(audioContext.currentTime);

        return osc;
      });
    },
    stop: function() {
      for (var i = 0; i < app.oscillators.length; i += 1) {
        app.oscillators[i].stop(audioContext.currentTime);
      }
    }
  }
  return app
};
```

These file modifications give your code the ability to create a gain node for each oscillator. The `play` method of the app object contains a map method that creates the gain nodes and sets the `gain.gain.value` property of each one to the value of the current object's `volume` property. All gain nodes are placed in an array that is assigned to `app.gainNodes`.

```
app.gainNodes = app.patchParams.map(function(val) {
  var gain = audioContext.createGain();
  gain.gain.value = val.volume;
  return gain;
});
```

The oscillators are then connected to the gain nodes in the second map method.

```
app.oscillators = app.patchParams.map(function(val, i) {

  var osc = audioContext.createOscillator();
  osc.type = val.type;
  osc.frequency.value = val.frequency;
  osc.detune.value = (val.frequency) + (id * 100);
  osc.connect(app.gainNodes[i]);
  app.gainNodes[i].connect(audioContext.destination);
  osc.start(audioContext.currentTime);

  return osc;
});
```

▌ Extend the JSON Object

The JSON object has only one "patch." You can extend it with as many patches as you like. The following code extends the object with a property (patch) named gameSound.

```
{
  "buzzFunk": [{
    "type": "sawtooth",
    "frequency": 65.25,
    "volume": 1
  }, {
    "type": "triangle",
    "frequency": 65.25,
    "volume": 1
  }, {

    "type": "sawtooth",
    "frequency": 67.25,
    "volume": 0.3
  }],
  "gameSound": [{
    "type": "square",
    "frequency": 100.25,
    "volume": 1
```

```
  }, {
    "type": "triangle",
    "frequency": 65.25,
    "volume": 1
  }, {

    "type": "sawtooth",
    "frequency": 67.25,
    "volume": 0.3
  }]
}
```

You then access the gameSound settings by loading them with apiReader.

```
var synth = apiReader("js/data.js", "gameSound");
```

▌ Summary

In this chapter, you learned how to query third-party web APIs, work with JSON files, and create your own web API to load patch data for a synthesizer. The application you created only begins to explore what is possible. For a challenge, try incorporating filters, LFOs, delays, and other settings. In the next chapter, you will learn about the future of JavaScript and various resources for continued learning.

25 The Future of JavaScript and the Web Audio API

In this book, you have learned the core concepts behind the JavaScript programming language and the Web Audio API. To keep from overcomplicating things, some parts of both the JavaScript language and the Web Audio API have been omitted. This chapter presents some of the areas that were skipped and provides you a few suggestions about what you can learn now to future-proof your new skills.

The Web Audio API 1.0

As of this writing, the Web Audio API has *not* reached version 1.0. This means that there are parts of the API that are either changing or have changed but are not implemented in web browsers. The following two sections talk more about this.

3D Spacial Positioning

In addition to the StereoPanner node, there are two other spacial positioning nodes. Both of these nodes allow for 3D style panning. One is called Panner and the other is called SpacialPanner. Panner has been recently deprecated. The replacement for Panner is SpacialPanner. As of this writing,

`SpacialPanner` has not been implemented in any web browsers. This makes it difficult to write about it and check the accuracy of code samples. And for this reason, we opted to omit a detailed explanation of `SpacialPanner` and present a general summary here.

The idea behind 3D spacial positioning is that sound is modified in relation to two objects in a three-dimensional space. The first object is a sound source that has its spacial positioning moved using `SpatialPanner`. The other object is called `SpatialListener` that represents a real-world human listener. The utility of this approach is that the `SpatialListener` object can be programmed to work with an avatar such as a video game character, where sound that is generated in a "virtual world" is perceived from a first-person perspective. Volume changes take place automatically based on the virtual "distance" between the `SpatialListener` and any sound-generating virtual objects. For added realism, filters, reverberation, and other effects can be programmed to change the characteristics of sound based on the perceived position of virtual objects. You can read about `SpatialPanner` at the following URL: https://www.w3.org/TR/webaudio/#the-spatialpannernode-interface.

You can read about the `SpatialListener` at this URL: https://www.w3.org/TR/webaudio/#idl-def-SpatialListener.

Raw Modification of Audio Buffer Data

The Web Audio API allows for the raw modification of audio data. You do this by either creating empty audio buffers and populating them with your own programmed data or by modifying buffers that already contain data such as audio file information. These modifications can be used to create custom effects and other useful things like noise generators. The node initially used for this was named `ScriptProcessor`, but this been deprecated and replaced with a node named `AudioWorker`. Unfortunately, as of this writing there are no web browsers that have implemented the `AudioWorker` node, so a detailed exploration of it has been omitted from this book. You can read about the `AudioWorker` node at this URL: https://developer.mozilla.org/en-US/docs/Web/API/Web_Audio_API#Audio_Workers.

Suggestions for Continued Learning

JavaScript 6

http://es6-features.org/(unofficial)

JavaScript 6, technically called ECMAScript 6 or commonly referred to as ES6, is the newest version of the JavaScript language and is currently being implemented in various JavaScript environments. The material in this book is focused on the ECMAScript 5 standard and is reflective of the majority of JavaScript in use around the world at the time of this writing. I suggest that you learn ES6 moving forward. ES6 has unique features such as block-scoped variables that build on the ES5 specification. Everything you have learned about ES5 is transferable to ES6.

node.js

https://nodejs.org

Node.js is a *server-side* JavaScript environment based on V8, which is the same JavaScript engine that runs Google Chrome. Instead of running JavaScript from a web browser, Node.js allows you to run JavaScript from the terminal on your computer. It can be used to automate computer tasks, run web servers, and communicate with databases.

The Web MIDI API

https://www.w3.org/TR/webmidi/

MIDI, which stands for Music Instrument Digital Interface, is a digital music instrument protocol created in 1982 by Dave Smith and Chet Wood. The Web MIDI API allows users to control and manipulate MIDI-equipped devices using web browsers.

Open Sound Control

http://opensoundcontrol.org/

According to their website, Open Sound Control (OSC) is "a protocol for communication among computers, sound synthesizers, and other multimedia devices that is optimized for modern networking technology." In other words, OSC is a protocol that facilitates the communication between hardware and software over a network.

Summary

In this chapter, you were presented with a list of options for continued learning. Even though JavaScript has been taught here in the context of working with audio, it is important to keep in mind that programming is a useful cross-disciplinary skill that you can use to solve many different types of problems.

Further Reading

- JavaScript: The Definitive Guide by David Flanagan.
- Understanding ECMAScript 6 by Nicholas C. Zakas.
- Programming JavaScript Applications: Robust Web Architecture with Node, HTML5, and Modern JS Libraries by Eric Elliott.
- You Don't Know JS Book Series by Kyle Simpson.
- Node.js the Right Way: Practical, Server-Side JavaScript That Scales by Jim R. Wilson.
- Web Audio API by Boris Smus.

Book Website

http://www.javascriptforsoundartists.com

Index

3D spacial positioning, 221–222

A

Abstraction, 129–135, 185–189
Addition assignment, 24–25
AJAX, 3, 207–209
Algebra rules, 18
Ambience, 151
Analyser node, 175–183
AND operator, 29
Animation, 107, 182
Anonymous functions, 48–49; *see also*
    Functions
API (application programming interface),
    3–4; *see also* Web Audio API
App interface, modifying, 81–84
Application, building, 71–89, 93–102
Application, refactoring, 108–110
Arguments, 16, 43–44
Arithmetic operators, 18, 23–25;
    see also Numbers
Arrays
    callback functions and, 53–54

for loops and, 36–37
frequency data arrays, 180–182
numbers and, 21–22
objects and, 60
track arrays, 197–206
Assignment operators, 11, 23–25; *see also*
    Operators
Asynchronous code execution, 118–120
Asynchronous JavaScript and XML
    (AJAX), 3, 207–209
Attack property, 166
AudioBatchLoader function,
    130–131, 134–135, 185–189
AudioContext() method, 65
AudioFileLoader function, 131–134,
    186–192, 198–200
Audio files
    abstracting, 129–135
    asynchronous code execution,
        118–120
    buffer, 116–120, 222
    compatibility issues, 118
    decoding, 116, 119

get requests, 116–120
importing, 117–120
impulse response files, 151–154
loading, 115–120, 129–135, 185–192, 198–200
modifying, 222
playing, 10, 115–120, 129–135
prerequisites for, 115–116
synchronous code execution, 118–120
XMLHttpRequest, 116–120
Audio input sources, 137–142, 155–167, 175–179, 183–185
Audio loader abstraction, 185–189
Audio loader library
creating, 121, 185
flexibility for, 185–189
modifying, 186–189
updating, 171, 183, 185
Audio parameters, 140–141, 171–174
Audio visualizations, creating, 175–183

B

Background color, 78–82, 86–87, 178, 203–206, 214
Bang operator, 28
Binary-coded decimal numbers, 176
Binary system, 176
Bin count, 177–182
Bind function, 62–64
Bins, 179–182
Biquad filter node
for audio filtering, 140–142
for designing equalizers, 144–149
types of, 144–147
using, 143–144
Bits, 176
Block-level element, 75–76, 84, 87–89
Boolean data type, 25–26
Boolean values, 25–29
Border, 84–85
Bound object, 62–64
Box model, 74
Browser setup view, 6
Buffer data, modifying, 222
Buffer, processing, 116–120
Buffer source node, 119–120
Bullet points, 86
Bytes, 176

C

Callback functions, 52–54
Case insensitivity, 16
CDN (content delivery network), 103–105
Centering elements, 87–89
Changeability, 13
Channel merger nodes, 159–160
Channel merging, 158–160
Channel splitting, 158–160
CharAt(), 15–17
Child selectors, 80
Chrome developer tools, 7–8, 10, 14, 78
Classes, 121–122
Class identifier, 81
Cloning objects, 60
Closures, 49–52
Code, 10–12
Code abstraction, 129–135
Code block, 36, 79
Code snippets, 6–7
Color selection, 78–82, 86–87, 178, 203–206, 214
Comments, 12, 72, 79
Comparison operators, 26–30; see also Operators
Compatibility issues, 118
Concat(), 21–22
Concatenation, 14–15, 20–22
Conditional statements, 31–35
Console.log(), 13–14
Constructors, 121, 125–128
Convolver node, 140, 151–155
Convolver reverb, 151–155
CSS (cascading style sheets)
app interface, 81–84
block-level elements, 87–89
border, 84–85
for building user interface, 77–89
bullet points, 86
buttons, 74–79
checking errors in, 77–78
child selectors, 80
code block, 79
color selection, 78–82, 86–87, 178, 203–206, 214
comments, 79
data structure of, 214–216
descendent selectors, 80
DOM programming, 91–93, 102

element selectors, 79
explanation of, 2–3, 74, 77–78
inline element, 84
with JQuery, 106–108
link element, 77
list element, 86
margins, 84–85, 87–89
method chaining, 107–108
padding, 84–85
selecting elements, 105
sequencer, 203–204
sliders, 74, 76–78
spectrum analyzer, 178

D

Data.js, 211–217, 220
Data, private, 124–125, 127
Data, query, 207–220
Data types, 11, 57–58
Decimal numbers, 19, 169, 176, 180
Delay node, 140, 161–164
Delete keyword, 188
Descendent selectors, 80
Destination, 9–10
Detune property, 69
Developer tools, 7–8, 10, 14, 78
Display interface, building, 181–182
Div element, 73, 75–76
Division assignment, 25
Document Object Model (DOM), 74
DOM programming
API methods, 92
building application, 93–102
CSS and, 91–93, 102
event listener, 99–100
explanation of, 74
frequency slider, 96–99
frequency spectrum analyzer, 181–183
HTML and, 74, 91–102
with JavaScript, 74, 91–102, 181
with JQuery, 103–113
nodes, 96, 100
selectors, 105–106, 111–112, 153
setInterval method, 97–101
simplifying, 103–113
start/stop text, 94–96
triggering oscillator, 93–94
Drum sequence, 191–206; see also
Sequencer

Dynamic compressor node, 165–167
Dynamic object extension, 123–124;
see also Objects
Dynamic range compression, 140, 165–167

E

Echo effects, 162
Effects
building blocks for, 141–142
echo effects, 162
effects box, 42–43
example of, 141
nodes for, 139–142
ping-pong effects, 163–164
slap back effects, 162–163
types of, 139–142
working with, 137–142
Elements
block-level elements, 75–76, 84, 87–89
centering, 87–89
changing, 106–107
div element, 73, 75–76
form element, 73–74, 76–78
heading element, 73
horizontal rule element, 73, 76
inline element, 75–76, 84
input element, 73–74, 76–78,
107–108, 110
link element, 77
list element, 73, 86
list item element, 73, 86
paragraph element, 73
parent element, 80, 86–87, 205
selecting, 79, 105
span element, 73, 75–76
storing, 105–106
unordered list element, 73, 81
Element selectors, 79, 105
Equality operator, 26–27
Equalizers, 137, 140, 142–149
Equal to operator, 27–28
Event listener
audio buffer, 120
DOM programming, 99–100
JQuery, 107–111
playback, 135, 217
tempo changes, 204–205
ExponentialRampToValueAtTime
method, 172

F

Factories, 121–128
Fast Fourier transforms (FFTs), 176, 179–182
File loader, 115–120, 129–135
File type compatibility, 118
Filter(), 53
Filter types, 144–147
Font color, 86–87
Font size, 86–87
Font type, 86–87
For in loop, 59–60
For loop, 35–37
Form element, 73–74, 76–78
Fourier analysis, 175–176
Frequency, changing, 97–99
FrequencyData array, 180–182
Frequency data, storing, 180–181
Frequency property, 69
Frequency slider, 96–99
Frequency spectrum analyzer, 176–183
Functions
    anonymous functions, 48–49
    arguments object, 43–44
    bind function, 62–64
    callback functions, 52–54
    closures, 49–52
    declaring variables, 46–50
    effects box, 42–43
    example of, 39–44
    explanation of, 39
    expressions for, 41
    hoisting, 46–48
    oscillator playback, 41–43
    parts of, 40–41
    recursion, 54–55
    scope concept, 44–47

G

Gain nodes, 138–139, 194
Get requests, 116–120
Getters, 124–125
Global object, 63–64
Global replace, 16
Global scope, 44–47, 64
Global variables, 46–50, 119
Google Chrome, 4–7; *see also* Chrome
    developer tools
Graphic equalizer, 143, 146–148; *see also*
    Equalizers

Greater than operator, 27–28
Grouping selectors, 80

H

Heading element, 73
"Hello Sound" application, 9–11
Hoisting variables, 46–48
Horizontal rule element, 73, 76
HTML (hypertext markup language)
    block-level elements, 75–76
    for building user interface, 71–77
    checking errors in, 72
    comments, 72
    data structure, 213
    DOM programming, 74, 91–102
    elements, 2, 71–74
    explanation of, 2–3, 71–74
    form element, 76–78
    impulse response files, 153
    inline element, 75–76
    input element, 76–78
    iTunes API, 210
    JQuery and, 105–108
    method chaining, 107–108
    selecting elements, 105
    sequencer, 202–203
    spectrum analyzer, 177–178
    tags, 2, 71–74
    templates, 72–73
    this keyword, 108
    tree structure, 74–75
    type attribute, 76–77, 107
    value attribute, 77

I

Identifiers, 81
id identifier, 81
If statement, 32–33
Immutability, 13
Impulse response files, 151–154
Inline element, 75–76, 84
In operator, 60
Input element, 73–74, 76–78, 107–108, 110
Input sources, 137–142, 155–167, 175–179,
    183–185
iTunes API, 208–210

J

JavaScript
    building application, 93–102

changing properties, 106–107
classes and, 121–122
data types, 11, 57–58
DOM programming, 74, 91–102, 181
explanation of, 1–2
future of, 221–223
getting started with, 9–22
impulse response files, 151–154
method chaining, 107–108
new keyword, 117, 125–126
object-oriented programming, 121–122
overview of, 1–8
setup view in browser, 4–6
spectrum analyzer, 176–177
strict mode for, 5, 63–64, 93
this keyword, 61–62, 108, 126
JavaScript 6, 222
JavaScript Object Notation, 208; *see also*
        JSON object
JQuery
    CDN and, 103–105
    changing properties, 106–107
    CSS and, 106–109
    DOM programming, 103–113
    event listener, 107–111
    explanation of, 103
    HTML and, 105–108
    method chaining, 107–108
    methods, 106
    onOff in, 112
    oscillator with, 108–109
    refactoring application, 108–110
    referencing, 104
    selecting elements, 105
    setInterval in, 111–112
    setup, 103–104
    spectrum analyzer, 176–177
    storing elements, 105–106
    this keyword, 108
    using, 105–113
JSON object
    data.js, 211–217, 220
    data structure, 213–216
    explanation of, 207–208
    extending, 219–220
    iTunes API, 208–210
    module.js, 215–219
    patches, 210–212, 216, 219–220
    playback, 216–217
    for web API, 210–217

K
Knee property, 166

L
Length property, 15, 17
Less than operator, 27–28
LinearRampToValueAtTime
        method, 173
Link element, 77
List bullet points, 86
List element, 73, 86
List item element, 73, 86
Local scope, 44–47
Logical AND operator, 29
Logical NOT operator, 29–30
Logical operators, 28–30
Logical OR operator, 29
Loops
    explanation of, 31–32
    for loop, 35–37
    for in loop, 59–60
    looping sounds, 170–171
    loop property, 170–171
    while loop, 37–38
Low-pass filter, 141

M
Mac setup view, 6
Map(), 53–54
Margins, 84–85, 87–89
Math.abs(), 20
Math.ceil(), 19
Math.floor(), 19
Math.max(), 19
Math methods, 18–20
Math.min(), 19
Math object, 18
Math.random(), 19–20
Merger nodes, 155, 158–160
Method chaining, 107–108
Metronome function, 194–205
Mixing channels, 138
Modification nodes, 139
Module.js, 215–219
Modulo assignment, 25
Mono channels, 159–160
Multiband equalizer, 140, 142; *see also*
        Equalizers
Multichannel files, 157–160

Multiplication assignment, 25
Music sequencer, 191–206; *see also* Sequencer
Mutability, 13

N

New keyword, 117, 125–126
Node graphs; *see also* Nodes
    buffer node source, 119–120
    effects nodes, 139–142
    example of, 141
    explanation of, 137–138
    gain nodes, 138–139
    input sources, 138
    modification nodes, 139
    for Web Audio API, 65–66, 137–142
Node.js, 223
Nodes
    analyser node, 175–183
    biquad filter node, 140–149
    buffer source node, 119–120
    channel merger nodes, 159–160
    channel splitting, 158–160
    convolver node, 140, 151–155
    delay node, 140, 161–164
    dynamic compressor node, 140, 165–167
    effects nodes, 139–142
    explanation of, 138–139
    future of, 221–223
    gain nodes, 138–139, 194
    merger nodes, 155, 158–160
    modification nodes, 139
    node graphs, 65–66, 137–142
    placement of, 138–139
    splitter nodes, 158–160
    stereo panner node, 140, 157–158
    for Web Audio API, 65–66, 137–142
Not equal to operator, 28
NOT operator, 29–30
Null, 12
Numbers
    algebra rules, 18
    arithmetic operators, 18, 23–25
    arrays and, 21–22
    decimals, 19, 169, 176, 180
    math methods, 18–20
    math object, 18
    precedent example, 18–20
    precedent rules, 18

Number-to-string conversion, 20

O

Object literals, 57–58, 117, 208, 212
Object-oriented programming, 121–122
Objects
    arrays and, 60
    bound object, 62–64
    classes and, 122
    cloning, 60–61
    data types, 57–64
    dynamic object extension, 123–124
    factories and, 122–124
    global object, 63–64
    literals, 57–58, 117, 208, 212
    looping through, 59–60
    method for, 60
    programming, 121–122
    property for, 60
    prototypal inheritance, 61–62
    prototype object, 126–128
Onended property, 67
OnOff selector, 93–101, 112
Open Sound Control (OSC), 223
Operand, 23
Operators
    addition assignment, 24–25
    arithmetic operators, 18, 23–25
    assignment operators, 11, 23–25
    bang operator, 28
    categories of, 23–25
    comparison operators, 26–30
    division assignment, 25
    equality operator, 26–27
    equal to operator, 27–28
    explanation of, 23–24
    greater than operator, 27–28
    in operator, 60
    less than operator, 27–28
    logical operators, 28–30
    modulo assignment, 25
    multiplication assignment, 25
    not equal to operator, 28
    operand, 23
    setInterval method, 24–25
    strict equality operator, 27
    strict not equal to operator, 28
    subtraction assignment, 25
OR operator, 29

Oscillators
 creating, 41–45, 66–69, 119–120
 detune property, 69
 frequency property, 69
 with JQuery, 108–109
 methods for, 66–67
 onended property, 67
 playback, 9–10, 32, 41–43, 66–67,
  93–94, 108–109
 properties of, 66–67
 refactoring application, 108–110
 restarting, 67–68
 start/stop text, 94–96
 stop method, 67–68
 triggering, 93–94
 type property, 68–69
 for variables, 12–13
 for Web Audio API, 9–10, 66–69

P

Padding, 84–85
Paragraph element, 73
Parametric equalizers, 143, 146–149
Parent element, 80, 86–87, 205
Ping-pong delay, 163–164
Playback
 audio files, 10, 115–120, 129–135
 audio parameters, 171–174
 convolver reverb, 153–154
 event listener, 135, 217
 explanation of, 4
 for JSON object, 216–217
 looping sounds, 170–171
 oscillator playback, 9–10, 32, 41–43,
  66–67, 93–94, 108–109
 for sequencer, 192, 197–202
Pop(), 21–22
Precedent example, 18–20
Primitive data types, 57
Private data, 124–125, 127
Property
 attack property, 166
 changing, 106–107
 detune property, 69
 explanation of, 17
 frequency property, 69
 knee property, 166
 length property, 15, 17
 loop property, 170–171
 onended property, 67

prototype property, 126–128
 ratio property, 166
 reduction property, 165–167
 release property, 166
 threshold property, 166
 type property, 68–69
Prototypal inheritance, 61–62
Prototype object, 126–128
Prototype property, 126–128
Push(), 21

Q

Query string, 209–210

R

Ratio property, 166
Recursion, 54–55
Reduction property, 165–167
Regular expressions, 16
Release property, 166
Replace(), 16
Resources, 8, 15, 151–152, 222–223
Reverb, 151–155

S

Scope concept, 44–47
Selectors
 child selectors, 80
 descendent selectors, 80
 DOM selectors, 105–106,
  111–112, 153
 element selectors, 79, 105
 grouping, 80
 storing, 105–106
Sequencer
 building, 191–206
 CSS for, 203–204
 grid elements, 202–206
 HTML for, 202–203
 interactivity for, 205–206
 metronome, 194–205
 playback, 192, 197–202
 rhythmic patterns, 192–193
 tempo changes, 192, 195–206
 timing clock, 193–204
 track arrays, 197–206
 user interface grid, 202–206
SetInterval method
 assignment operators, 24–25
 DOM programming, 97–101

JQuery, 111–112
rhythmic patterns, 192–193
SetTargetAtTime() method, 173
Setters, 124–125
SetTimeout method, 192–197, 199–201
SetValueAtTime method, 172
SetValueCurveAtTime() method, 173–174
Shift(), 21–22
Single-band equalizer, 143, 148; *see also* Equalizers
Single mono channels, 159–160
Slap back effects, 162–163
Slice(), 16–17
Spacial planner node, 221–222
Span element, 73, 75–76
Spatial listener node, 221–222
Speakers, 138
Spectrum analyzer, connecting, 181–183
Spectrum analyzer, creating, 176–183
Splitter nodes, 158–160
Start method, 170–171
Step sequencer, 191–206; *see also* Sequencer
Stereo panner node, 140, 157–158, 221–222
Stop method, 67–68
Strict equality operator, 27
Strict mode, 5, 63–64, 93
Strict not equal to operator, 28
Strict string, 93–97, 100, 109
String data types, 11, 14–16
String methods, 15–17
Strings
    case insensitivity, 16
    data types, 11, 14–16
    global replace, 16
    length property, 15, 17
    manipulating, 14–17
    methods, 15–17
    number-to-string conversion, 20
    regular expressions, 16
    resources for, 15
    values for, 16–17
    variables and, 14–17
Sublime Text, 4–6, 115
Subtraction assignment, 25
Switch statement, 33–34
Synchronous code execution, 118–120
Synthesizer patch data, 210–212, 216, 219–220

T

Template folders, 4–5
Templates, 72–73
Tempo, changing, 192, 195–206
Ternary statement, 34–35
Text size, 86–87
Third-party web APIs, 207–220
This keyword, 61–62, 108, 126
Threshold property, 166
Time
    audio parameter methods, 171–174
    looping sounds, 170–171
    start method, 170–171
    timing clock, 169–170, 193–204
    working with, 169–174
ToLowerCase(), 15
ToUpperCase(), 15
Track arrays, 197–206
Troubleshooting tips, 8–9
Type attribute, 76–77
Type property, 68–69
Typestyle, 86–87

U

Unordered list element, 73, 81
Unshift(), 21–22
User interface (UI)
    building, 71–89
    CSS for, 77–89
    explanation of, 71–72
    HTML for, 71–77
    modifying, 81–84

V

Value attribute, 77, 106, 108, 110
Values
    assigning, 11, 13, 23–26
    Boolean values, 25–29
    for strings, 16–17
Variables
    assigning values to, 11, 13, 23–26
    assignments, 10–14
    changeability of, 13
    concatenation of, 14–15
    creating, 10
    data type of, 17–18
    declaring, 46–50
    global variables, 46–50, 119
    hoisting, 46–48

immutability of, 13
mutability of, 13
names, 13–14
null value, 12
oscillator for, 12–13
overwriting, 13
strings and, 14–17
undefined value, 12
understanding, 10–11
waveforms, 10–14, 17–18, 21
Visualizations, creating, 175–183
Volume control, 138

W

W3C (World Wide Web Consortium), 72, 77
Waveforms
  changing, 99–100
  outline for, 101–102
  selecting, 99–102
  types of, 10–14, 41–44, 68–69, 99–102
  variables, 10–14, 17–18, 21
Web Audio API
  audio output, 9–10
  creating, 210–212
  destination, 9–10
  explanation of, 3–4
  features of, 65–66
  future of, 221–223
  getting started with, 9–22
  "Hello Sound" application, 9–11
  nodes for, 65–66, 137–142
  oscillators, 9–10, 66–69
  resources for, 8
  variables, 10–11
  waveforms, 11–14, 17–18, 21
Web MIDI API, 223
While loop, 37–38
Windows setup view, 6
Work environment, 4–6

X

XML (Extensible Markup Language), 207;
  see also AJAX
XMLHttpRequest, 116–120, 131–133,
  152–153, 207–209

Z

Zero-based index, 16, 43